AREAS OF FOG

AREAS OF FOG

WILL DOWD

Will Dowd

Etruscan Press

Etruscan Press
Wilkes University
84 West South Street
Wilkes-Barre, PA 18766
(570) 408-4546

WILKES UNIVERSITY

www.etruscanpress.org

Published 2017 by Etruscan Press
Printed in the United States of America
Cover image: Cloud Cleaner 1999 © Robert and Shana ParkeHarrison,
    Courtesy Catherine Edelman Gallery, Chicago
Cover design by Julianne Popovec
Interior design and typesetting by Susan Leonard
The text of this book is set in Garamond.

First Edition

16 17 18 19 20 5 4 3 2 1

Library of Congress Cataloging-in-Publication Data

Names: Dowd, Will, 1984- author.
Title: Areas of fog / Will Dowd.
Description: First edition. | Wilkes-Barre, PA : Etruscan Press, 2017.
Identifiers: LCCN 2017008385 | ISBN 9780997745535 (paperback)
Subjects: | BISAC: LITERARY COLLECTIONS / Essays. | NATURE / Weather. |
  HISTORY / United States / State & Local / New England (CT, MA, ME, NH, RI,
  VT).
Classification: LCC PS3604.O93846 A6 2017 | DDC 814/.6--dc23
LC record available at https://lccn.loc.gov/2017008385

Please turn to the back of this book for a list of the sustaining funders of Etruscan Press.

This book is printed on recycled, acid-free paper.

For Kim Lourenco,
who lit the candles
when the lights went out

Poets are always taking the weather so personally.

— J. D. Salinger

CONTENTS

AREAS OF FOG

OVERTURE

ALL THE WEATHERMEN of New England go mad eventually.

After a few decades spent attempting to predict the unpredictable, they succumb to a kind of meteorological nihilism and wander out of the studio mid-broadcast, muttering to themselves, and can be seen a week later selling wilted roses on the side of the highway.

It's not the seasonal anarchy—all those balmy Christmases and washed-out Junes—but rather the perverse changeability of our daily weather, the adolescent moodiness of our sun and sky, that finally unravels the sweater of their sanity.

"In the spring, I have counted one hundred and thirty-six different kinds of weather inside of four and twenty hours," Mark Twain, a Hartford resident for seventeen years, once quipped.

Yet while they may be doomed to fail, we don't mock our weathermen. Even though we see them for what they are—oracles draped in sheep entrails—we don't change the channel. We listen politely to their forecast.

And then we talk about it.

In New England, the weather is all we talk about, especially when we have nothing to talk about.

Lately, I've been suffering from writer's block.

It's a serious disease.

It struck Twain in the midst of composing *The Adventures of Huckleberry Finn.* After scratching 400 handwritten pages over the course of a single summer, the author suddenly found he could not write another word. For years, Huck and Jim were left stranded on the river, paddling in place. Eventually, Twain found his cure: a refreshing 16-month trip through Europe.

I'm hoping to find my cure closer to home.

Over the next year, I plan to keep a weather journal, a kind of running retrospective forecast.

It will be accurate, for one thing. I can say it rained today with 100% certainty, for example, because I swallowed some of it.

But I have another reason for glancing at the near meteorological past. Writers only ever use the atmosphere for atmosphere. They never give the weather its literary due.

"Of course weather is necessary to a narrative of human experience," Twain wrote. "But it ought to be put where it will not be in the way; where it will not interrupt the flow of the narrative."

So here's a place just for the weather: a snow globe without a figurine or a monument. Just the weather.

And maybe, probably, my reflection in the glass.

JANUARY

LONDON TOWN

NOTHING WAS HAPPENING this week, weather-wise. Monday was mild—a fugitive March day hiding out in mid-January—while Tuesday left so little impression on my mind that I could not swear in a court of law the day actually transpired.

Then the fog rolled in.

It happened on Wednesday night, when no one was looking. Dusk fell, the mercury dropped, and suddenly the whole east coast of Massachusetts was saturated in abject eeriness.

I walked outside and found reality suspended, the everyday world dissolved in a cataract gloom.

Somewhere ahead of me in the white murk, I heard the hollow sound of a glass bottle rolling on its side. It came to a jangling stop against a curb, then began rolling again, back the way it had come.

All considered, the fog gave me the haunting sense that strange things were about to happen. I felt like a character on the first page of a novel.

I wasn't alone.

"I feel like we're in *Sherlock Holmes*," my grandmother remarked when I saw her on Thursday. She was right, of course. It was fine weather for fishing a body from the Thames or swinging your cane at a street urchin.

If anyone recognized the literary merits of fog, it was the Victorian authors, who practically mass-produced the stuff. It was their way of dropping a veil on their hyper-rational, industrialized metropolis.

In one Sherlock Holmes story, the bored detective condemns London criminals for not taking advantage of a weeklong fog. "The thief or the murderer could roam London on such a day as the tiger does the jungle," Holmes says. "It is fortunate for this community that I am not a criminal."

Interestingly, at least to an English major, fog always seems to gather on the first page of these stories.

It pours through Scrooge's keyhole at the start of *A Christmas Carol*, swirls with metaphoric import at the beginning of *Bleak House*, and even appears in its cousin form—marsh-mist—to blind Pip at the dawn of *Great Expectations*.

And that's just Dickens.

Fog belongs on the first page of novels. That's how literature comes to us. It emerges from the ghostly haze of the blank page, and if you take just a few steps into it, you lose sight of who you were and where you came from.

Take Sherlock's advice to Watson: bring a revolver.

BARE BONES

IT'S ALWAYS THIS time of year—when the snowstorms have begun to bleed into each other and the air, just teething in December, now has real bite—that my pale Irish skin loses its ivory sheen and becomes actually translucent, and you can see my major organs quivering like koi fish under a layer of ice.

It was a week of slow, steady accumulation.

On Saturday, we had snowflakes the size of movie tickets. On Wednesday, they flew in our eyes like flicked ash. By Friday, every window in New England was like the frame of an Andrew Wyeth winter landscape.

Andrew Wyeth loved this time of year. The painter, who died five years ago this week, spent most of his life on long walks with his paper and sable brushes, trying to find the right snowbank to sit on.

"God, I've frozen my ass off painting snow scenes!" he once supposedly said.

It's one thing to be a plein-air artist in the south of France, but anyone who shoveled their driveway this week has to respect a man who painted mittenless in this weather for decades.

For Wyeth, exposure to the elements was essential to his art. It got him out of his head. "When I'm alone in the woods, across these fields, I forget all about myself, I don't exist," he said. "I'd just as soon walk around with no clothes on."

I used to think Wyeth chose his favorite subject—isolated barn in a sea of snow—mostly to save paint. Some of his finished watercolors are more than seventy percent untouched paper.

But the more I look at his wintry landscapes, the more they seem to take on an otherworldly glow. For Wyeth, the white space of winter was not a shortcut. It was a mystery.

"I prefer winter and fall, when you can feel the bone structure in the landscape—the loneliness of it," the painter said. "Something waits beneath it—the whole story doesn't show."

This is especially true for "Snow Birds," a Wyeth watercolor recently slated to be auctioned at Christie's for $500,000.

Shortly before being sold, it was discovered to be a fake. (You can always expect a flurry of forgeries in the wake of an artist's death.)

There are small details that give it away.

For example, Wyeth painted pine trees by laying down an undercoat of green, then trickling black branches over it—not the reverse, as seen in the fraud.

Also, the forger was too stiff in his brushwork. The shadows are labored; the hillside is stilted; even the signature is too neat. Wyeth, who painted with fingers that ached to be back in his warm pockets, was all speed and dash with his brushes.

No, this winter landscape was not painted by Andrew Wyeth. It was not painted by someone whose hands were cold.

LATITUDES

I SPENT THE past two weeks flat on my back—the result of a slipped disc—and, consequently, my contact with the weather has been limited, though I did crawl from room to room each afternoon to lie in puddles of surprisingly warm sunlight like a cat, all the while staring at the ceiling and working fitfully on my living will, which a combination of boredom and the sudden simulacrum of old age spurred me to tackle.

It wasn't so bad.

Eventually the random swirls on the ceiling assembled into compelling shapes, and of course there's a quiet joy in planning one's funeral.

Only last Monday, when I hobbled to the doctor's office like the Elephant Man, did I directly experience the weather. At three o'clock the sun was already low, impaled on some branches. The sky was a filthy blue, and it was freezing out. My bare knuckles felt as if they were in a vice, though I barely noticed due to the summer lightning of nerve pain in my left leg. Funny how separate pains in the body vie for conscious attention like claimants to a medieval throne.

"Why is this happening?" I asked the nurse practitioner.

"Well," she said, "your lumbar vertebrae have become compressed and—"

"No, I mean why is this happening *to me*?"

It's the existential question that all New Englanders ask themselves in late January. We stand at (or lie beneath) a sunny window, attempting to bask in secondhand warmth, and ask ourselves the question: why is winter happening to me?

Why do I live here?

Voluntarily?

What complex web of self-sabotaging life decisions led me to take up residence at 42° North, a latitude which, if the Northern Hemisphere had a spine, would correspond roughly to the first lumbar vertebrae, the kidney-shaped bone giving me such trouble?

Come to think of it, why is there a winter at all?

Why does the Earth even teeter on its axis?

Why can't it always be summer?

But these are childish questions. It's no use arguing with the weather or trying to wish it away. Like a funeral, life goes on. Rain or shine.

February

AN INNER SCHEME

THIS WEEK I planned to write about prognostication, a theme suggested (no surprise here) by the punctual reemergence of Punxsutawney Phil, the celebrity rodent who's been predicting the weather since 1887, though of course it's not the original Punxsutawney—given the average lifespan of a captive groundhog, Phil has had more incarnations than the Dalai Lama. Then I was going to address the lead-up to Wednesday's early morning snow bestowal, when dozens of Massachusetts superintendents (a notoriously skeptical order) canceled school before a single flake had fallen. Then I was going to mention the chilling prophecy of my physical therapist ("Snow means shoveling, and shoveling means more business for us"). And then I thought I would discuss the animal tracks I saw Tuesday night (a groundhog's?) with particular reference to the Dogon medicine men of Mali who divined the future in paw prints left by the desert fox in the sand at night. Finally, I was going to conclude with my own Wednesday morning walk through the superintendent-vindicating snow and how I turned at one point and looked back at the receding trail of my boot prints and wondered what they foretold.

But I don't want to write about all that. It seems too predictable somehow. Too predetermined.

What I really want to write about are these icicles hanging outside my window—the glittering daggers that would make the perfect murder weapon, if you think about it.

Yet now I have a new problem. Any attempt to describe an icicle sweating in afternoon sun is haunted and taunted by Vladimir Nabokov, who did it better, who did it best:

"I had stopped to watch a family of brilliant icicles drip-dripping from the eaves.... I did not chance to be watching the right icicle when the right drop fell. There was a rhythm, an alternation in the dripping that I found as teasing as a coin trick."

It's as if certain features of New England weather are copyrighted by certain writers:

Dickinson has a trademark on that slant of afternoon light.

Frost owns ice-bowed boughs.

And Nabokov has an incontestable claim on melting icicles.

The passage above, by the way, comes from Nabokov's short story "The Vane Sisters," in which a French professor in Cambridge, Massachusetts fears he is being haunted, and unconsciously controlled, by the ghosts of two sisters—one a former student, one a former lover.

When the story was rejected by *The New Yorker*, Nabokov was not pleased.

"I feel that *The New Yorker* has not understood 'The Vane Sisters' at all," he wrote to the editor. Didn't she recognize that the first letters of each word in the last paragraph of the story formed an acrostic? "I am really very disappointed that you, such a subtle and loving reader, should not have seen the inner scheme of my story."

"Subtle and loving"—that's the kind of reader Nabokov wanted and expected. A reader so enraptured by his prose, so confident in his godlike resourcefulness, so in love with him, in short, that he or she would always be watching the right icicle when the drop fell.

Who needs that kind of love? That level of adoration? I don't. All I need are these icicles in the window.

Vivid, lucent, antically dripping icicles, menacing iridescent rapiers, yards over us, glinting ominously, towering nobly, oozing tears, hypnotic, imperial, now glowing orange, now melting elegantly.

Carry On

According to the news, it's a war out there.

This week, a blizzard dragged its icy talons up the East Coast, severing power lines and snapping utility poles.

Winter Storm Pax, apparently named by a sardonic Latin scholar working at The Weather Channel, laid siege to Atlanta and entombed Charleston. The news makes it sound like North Carolina died.

When the storm finally reached Massachusetts on Thursday, it just stood there and delivered a long, commanding lecture on the nature of slush.

In Boston, an entire street was shut down when a 6-foot icicle fell three stories and almost harpooned a pedestrian.

It's possible that, for once, the weathermen aren't exaggerating: it *is* a war out there.

Speaking of which, I've always thought a decent dissertation could be written on the so-called Southie Parking Wars.

There's a tradition in South Boston: if you dig out a public parking space after a major snowstorm, you temporarily own it, so long as you mark your territory by leaving some kind of object in the excavated space. Whenever a territorial claim is violated, tires get slashed, windows get smashed, and, sometimes, heads get bashed.

It's been called a gentleman's agreement, and, given the mayor's tacit consent, the whole thing has a vague semi-legal status.

More than anything, I'm interested in what people choose to leave in their shoveled-out spaces. While it's often cones, which have an air of officialdom, you also see a lot of beach chairs, open and turned toward the street. These chairs work because they play a mind game. You can't help but imagine the owner sitting there like a ghost, watching intently, a tire iron resting across his knees.

In fact, it's all mind games. You often see children's bicycles, which are good for sympathy.

I once saw an old toilet—who's gonna touch that?

And then there's the really small, frail gestures—ironing boards, empty shopping bags, gloves—which work by reverse psychology. Whoever has the audacity to leave an old shoe must be a trained killer.

The ultimate power play, I've always thought, would be to shovel out your space and then erect a small house of cards.

Like I said, it's a war out there.

And there's more to come. Tonight, my swathe of Massachusetts is forecast to receive another bombardment of 8 to 10 inches. Already tiny flakes are arriving like light infantry.

The weathermen are beginning to sound like Winston Churchill, whose wartime speeches gave comfort to the Britons huddled around their wireless sets as bombs fell from the sky.

Churchill used to spend eight hours at a stretch working on his broadcasts, and his best lines still echo today on coffee mugs and specialty greeting cards. A new book, however, suggests that the public wasn't as inspired by Churchill's speeches as we imagine in retrospect.

They didn't like his long-windedness, they couldn't bear his fondness for double negatives, and there was a widespread suspicion that during his speeches he wasn't not drunk.

I'd like to do something—or at least say something—to help you all get through this winter. This war.

I think I'll leave you with these words.

Keep calm and—well, you know the rest.

GENESIS

IT'S BEEN A winter of naming. Every week the weather-indus-trial complex introduces and circulates a new buzzword for a weather phenomenon that has always existed ("Bombogenesis" is having its moment), while The Weather Channel has gone rogue and begun naming blizzards. They're not even proceeding through the alphabet. It's chaos.

But is it surprising?

Sooner or later, winter was bound to be branded, or at least hashtagged, relabeled and resold by the paranoid-delusional 24-hour news cycle as yet another sign of the Apocalypse, which itself has an impressive catalog of names—Doomsday, Armageddon, End Times, Eschaton, Ragnarök.

That last one, Ragnarök, refers to a climactic contretemps between Norse gods, a clash to be preceded by a mighty winter and a wolf swallowing the sun. It's all described in a 13th-century compilation of Icelandic poetry, and, according to one group of Viking experts, it's scheduled to occur this weekend.

Yet despite the media's best effort to trademark various aspects of the season, we still lack a basic wintry vocabulary.

We still have no name for the first labored swipe of wind-shield wipers over morning frost.

We still have no name for the mist that rises off the shoul-ders of melting snowmen like their departing souls.

We still have no name for the evening snow that falls like Pompeian ash, redly illuminated by the brake lights of infinite traffic on your commute home.

We still have no name for the desolate winter rain that fell on Wednesday, the kind that would be depicted as thin vertical lines in a Japanese woodblock, nor for the sideways, abacus-like sliding of freezing raindrops across the brim of an open umbrella.

And still, still we have no name for a balmy February afternoon, such as the one we had on Thursday, when the sun comes back to you like a lost dog from childhood and lays its golden paw on your chest.

MARCH

THE LIGHTS OF HEALTH

THEY SAY MARCH comes in like a lion, and this year they're right. We had a whiteout last Wednesday (I skidded home in four-wheel drive on a tread of Hail Marys), then a Nor'easter that never materialized (some believe it's still out there, biding its time), and finally temperatures so unseasonably, unreasonably cold that everyone in the Greater Boston area, fearing winter might be permanent, scurried around in a state of near panic, as if a lion had cleared the fence at Franklin Park Zoo and begun picking off pedestrians one by one.

But then things changed.

This morning, the sun remembered to bring actual warmth with it. There was an ocean smell on the wind. A couple of hawks, back from the Florida Keys, rolled around in the bright wind, scanning backyards for a Pekingese let out to pee. I heard a sound that was strange yet somehow familiar, like the looped melancholy tones of a long-forgotten arcade game. It was birdsong.

Most critically, it was a few degrees warmer. That doesn't sound like much, but a few degrees can hinge a season just as surely as it can unhinge a mind.

Earlier this week, I ran a low-grade fever. The slight change to my microclimate altered the landscape around me with frightening, hallucinatory efficiency.

"[H]ow astonishing," Virginia Woolf wrote, "when the lights of health go down, the undiscovered countries that are then disclosed, what wastes and deserts of the soul a slight attack of influenza brings to view, what precipices and lawns sprinkled with bright flowers a little rise of temperature reveals."

Woolf would know. She suffered her whole life from mysterious, unexplained fevers. She would lie in bed and listen to the sparrows speaking in Greek outside her window.

Her diary, which is full of gaps, tracks her periods of convalescence like a thermometer. In the most moving entries, she resurfaces from her sickbed, laments how much time she has lost, and resolves to pick up the thread of her novel-in-progress.

It's probably a sacrilege, but I prefer Woolf's twenty-six-year diary to her novels. She was a diligent chronicler of her own life, jotting down anything, everything. The only experience she would not describe in her diary, she told a friend, was her own death.

Naturally, the diary is full of weather.

Here she is in January: "All frost. Still frost. Burning white. Burning blue." And in June: "Perfect summer weather. It's like an invalid who can look up and take a cup of tea." And in September: "Hot weather; a wind blowing. The substance gone out of everything."

Even in her last entry, Woolf was careful to note the "curious sea side feeling in the air today."

A few days later she filled her pockets with stones and walked into the River Ouse.

It was March.

THIS FLOATING WORLD

I FIND IT hard, impossible really, not to see the weather on my birthday as God weighing in on things. I turned thirty on Wednesday. It rained heavily.

The weather this week was more of the same. Despite several days that thought about being warm, the winter cold kept reasserting itself, returning in the night to paint the town with a layer of black ice that had radiologists working overtime. There were bitter winds, night terror commutes, and Thursday flurries that served no discernible purpose.

One doesn't usually hear the word "evil" associated with the weather, but New Englanders have begun resorting to Manichaean language.

And who can blame us? Winter is like a maniacal mayor who keeps extending his term limits.

Perhaps the word "evil" is too strong for the weather, but how else can we describe the spiritual acid that is late winter rain?

I suppose we should look to the Japanese, whose poetry is the greatest repository of written weather in existence, a fact that has somehow escaped the notice of weathermen, who almost never incorporate haiku into the forecast.

The Japanese have a word for winter confinement (*fuyu-gomori*), moonlit night (*tsukiyo*), and shimmering summer air (*kagerō*).

They also have a word for late winter rain—*shigure*.

My favorite use of *shigure* comes from the little-known haiku poet Shida Yaba (1662-1740), who wrote:

> In this floating world
> a voice calls—
> winter shower

Yaba composed these lines on his deathbed. It was customary for haiku poets to jot down—or at least dictate—a haiku in their final moments of life.

I enjoy writing to a deadline as much as anyone, but talk about pressure. Imagine trying to concentrate on leaving this earthly plane while a crowd of students, eager with brush and paper, leans in around you, listening intently to your labored breathing, hoping to net a flutter of brilliance on the wind of your final exhalation.

Truth be told, the lines above are actually Yaba's second-to-last haiku. His last haiku was just plain bad, so his students—and now his readers—pretend it never happened.

We have to look out for each other.

OFF-SEASON

THIS WEEK, WHILE the Greater Boston area nursed a municipal hangover, courtesy of St. Patrick's Day, we survived a stretch of what I like to call parking lot weather—cold, blustery days when the endless motorcade of low-scudding clouds mirrors the geometric recession and metaphysical emptiness of a strip mall parking lot.

That is, until this morning, when the winter finally broke.

The sun rose like a soprano's Hallelujah.

I got into my car and drove with the windows down for the first time in five months. For some unexplained reason, after a long period of cryogenic gloom, driving with the windows down is the only thing that can bring me back to life.

The sky was a pale blue, save for the band of ultramarine at the top of my new windshield. (The old one cracked last week like thawing pond ice.) Somehow there were a few autumn leaves left to run over. The speed limit seemed out-of-season.

I was listening to Bach's Mass in B minor as remixed by the potholes of Route 3A. I usually don't care for liturgical music—anything played on the church organ sounds to my ears like a priest's ringtone—but somehow Bach's holy strains shone through.

Bach hated when the weather turned nice. As a kapellmeister, he depended on funeral masses—one a day, on average—to supplement his salary. Mild weather meant fewer corpses, and fewer corpses meant fewer funerals. I can just imagine Bach scowling as the first warm breeze of spring gusted through the narrow streets of Leipzig.

It's not a very attractive image, I admit, but I forgive the cantankerous choirmaster. After all, he and death were old acquaintances. When he was nine, Bach lost both his parents. (As a member of the local *chorus musicus*, he was obliged to sing as their caskets were lowered by ropes into unmarked graves.) He later lost three brothers, his first wife, and twelve of his twenty children before they reached the age of three. If anyone could accuse death of slacking off, it was Bach.

Soon my joyride brought me to Nantasket Beach, where the decrepit carousel and ice cream stands were still boarded up for the winter, waiting to be resurrected on Easter weekend.

I parked and walked cautiously onto the glowing beach. It was empty except for a black lab who trotted by, grinning and dripping seawater, dragging his leash in the sand.

For about ten seconds, it was nice.

Then a wave of darkness swept the beach. I looked up. Someone had blown out the sun; it smoldered behind a veil of clouds like a snuffed wick. A complex chemical reaction took place as the Atlantic frothed, then purpled. A raindrop hit me between the eyes.

I trudged back to my car and peeled out of the seaside parking lot, my speakers blasting a plea for divine mercy in B minor.

DEVIL WINDS

SO MUCH FOR going out like a lamb.

This week a blizzard interred Cape Cod, sending tail-winds to flog the Greater Boston area. The gales brought down branches and sent trucks fishtailing on the highway. They woke everyone in the middle of the night with otherworldly moans. On Wednesday, as if blowing on a campfire, they accelerated a blaze on Beacon Street. Two firefighters were tragically killed. It felt like anything could happen.

All this howling weather makes me think of the Santa Anas, the "devil winds" that afflict Los Angeles this time of year. They are notorious for fanning wildfires and, according to local legend, making people temporarily insane.

I have never personally felt the hot breath of the Santa Anas on the back of my neck, but I have encountered them time and again in my reading life. They're always blowing through the hardboiled fiction of Southern California.

The novelist Raymond Chandler, whose famous detective roamed the streets of his beloved and behated Los Angeles, captured the phenomenon better than anyone. His early story, "Red Wind," famously opens:

> There was a desert wind blowing that night. It
> was one of those hot dry Santa Anas that come
> down through the mountain passes and curl your

hair and make your nerves jump and your skin itch. On nights like that every booze party ends in a fight. Meek little wives feel the edge of the carving knife and study their husbands' necks.

While many of Chandler's stories became fodder for mid-century film noir, Hollywood producers refused to touch "Red Wind." I don't blame them: how could you ever reproduce the subcutaneous angst of the "devil winds" on film?

On Friday, I walked through the cleverly devised wind tunnel that is the MIT campus. (I lived in Cambridge for a year and my hair hasn't laid flat since.) An anxious Atlantic wind was gusting off the Charles River—you could practically hear the rowers cursing. It swept down Memorial Drive, looped around the shining nuclear reactor, and rolled up the flags commemorating the site where the MIT police officer was ambushed by the Marathon bombers.

I ducked into a sandwich shop, ordered something on sourdough and sat by the window where I could watch pedestrians chase their hats.

I thought about Boston—my city, for better or worse—and how much it's changed in the past decade, ever since it replaced Los Angeles as the go-to backdrop for noir cinema. Strange things happen to a city when it sees itself on film. It becomes self-conscious. Its charm turns to shtick. Its soul becomes a brand. And when the cameras pack up and head back west, it does what every washed-up celebrity does: reality television.

Eventually I noticed a crowd of people gathered on the street, their necks craned, their phones held aloft. I walked outside, turned around and looked up. The top floor of the building was on fire.

Within minutes the news choppers were circling overhead, battling crosswinds. They inched ever closer to the belching black smoke like moths drawn to a flame.

I reached for my phone.

APRIL

ORANGE PEELS

EARLIER THIS WEEK, I stood on the warm sands of New Smyrna Beach. While the Florida sun searched for a chink in my 100 SPF, I watched my friend drift lazily out to sea on the rolling carpet of a rip current. The lifeguard, who'd been whistling like a lunatic for minutes, grabbed a bullhorn and barked dire warnings. A hundred sunbathers lifted their heads to see what was the matter. "She'll be fine," I told the lifeguard. "She hiked the Appalachian trail, alone." Sure enough, my friend started swimming sideways, then kicked her way to shore, wringing out her hair as she emerged from the waves, looking bored, if anything.

Florida is as much a part of the New England winter as burst pipes. We all head for the Sunshine State at some point. Even if we have to hike there, alone.

It's a tradition.

Even hard-up Irish immigrants in the early 1900's made the trek from Boston. I know this because I have a trove of letters written between my great-grandmother Nora and her cousin Mary.

(I'm not sure how I ended up with these letters. I vaguely remember hearing that Nora was a voracious reader partial to Shakespeare and the possessor of a sharp wit that she declined to muzzle.)

In the winter of 1913, Mary got a job as a waitress at a hotel near New Smyrna Beach.

"The climate here is beautiful," she wrote to Nora. "The grass is so green and there are great big fields that we cross on our way to the beach. I eat about 15 oranges a day. We can pluck them off the tree when walking along the roads. They are as common here as crab apples in the harvest in Ireland."

I like to think of Mary walking the same Florida beach as me on her day off, reading Nora's letters while sitting on a dune, peeling an orange.

My friends and I stayed at a house in Deland, about thirty minutes inland. Geckos skittered over mesh screens. Catfish lurked in a backyard lake. After dark, the lake became the stage for a late-night symphony with a brooding string section of Palmetto bugs and a chorus of bullfrogs, whose grunted mating calls serve as definitive proof of erotic subjectivity.

Three or four times the first night, I thought I heard knuckles rapping on my windowpane.

The next morning, when I walked outside, a Sandhill Crane approached me on dainty, backward-bending legs, bowed slightly, then glared at me expectantly. He had a stripe of neon red war paint on his forehead and a beak like a bayonet.

I refused to give him a piece of my bagel. He tiptoed away, as if from the scene of a crime. I knew he'd been the one rapping at my window. Poe had a raven; I had a Sandhill Crane.

Of course, Florida is more than just a superabundance of sun and species. The air itself is a substance, a primordial soup in which everything swims. In Florida, things feel connected. The humidity is metaphysical. The Spanish moss swings eerily. There are legends, ghosts. I dipped one foot in De Leon Springs—the conical green pool rumored to be Ponce's long-sought Fountain of Youth. I'll let you know if one of my feet fails to age.

My friends and I made a pilgrimage to Cassadaga, a small, isolated town inhabited almost exclusively by psychics and mediums who, despite the sticky heat, wear tan suits and floral dresses.

We soon found ourselves sitting quietly in folding chairs inside a church hall, wondering if the medium pacing the room would alight on our lost, loitering ancestors.

I got picked, of course.

The medium saw someone bobbing beside me—a rather heavyset and opinionated older woman who kept offering me phantom books.

I'm sorry, I said, but all my female relatives are still on this side of the veil—and frighteningly thin.

Only later, on the plane back to chilly, sane New England, did I think of Nora and wonder about her waistline.

I did some digging when I got home and came across an old photo.

Out of respect and fear, I'll keep my metaphysical conclusions to myself.

NARCISSUS

JUST A QUICK note to say that spring doesn't care about us.

It certainly doesn't care about human time.

It keeps its own clock, and it comes when it comes.

Yes, spring arrived this week after a final, undignified coating of snow on Wednesday morning, but not because the spokes of the Gregorian and liturgical calendars seemed to align serendipitously—it doesn't care that Sunday is Easter, or that Monday is the first anniversary of the Boston Marathon bombing, or that Tuesday is the tenth anniversary of my near-death experience (crosswalk, minivan).

It doesn't care about the theme of resurrection.

Spring is an inhuman affair. A paroxysm of Nature. A manic procedure that operates beneath our perception like cellular regeneration.

And yet we feel it—the shadowy intuition of a hundred million hands, tiny and invisible, pushing upwards and outwards, all culminating in the shuddering eruption of a daffodil.

I once had a poetry professor with the wild hair and chunky rings of a fortune teller.

During a class one April afternoon, while the first wave of pollen was dusting the campus outside, her eyes unfocused and she wondered aloud, "How many more springs will each of you get?"

It was the kind of carpe diem sentiment one is liable to hear in a poetry class. But the motto didn't work its revitalizing magic on me.

It never does.

Spring is here, but it doesn't care about me, or you, or poetry.

We don't seize the day.

The day seizes us.

BEACH WALK

I'M WALKING WOLLASTON Beach. It's late April, so there's no chance of a tan and the water would kill me in seconds, but it's pleasant enough—the air is warm, the tide pools have a mother-of-pearl sheen, and, aside from the stubble of Boston, the horizon has a clean-shaven feel.

Every fifty yards or so, I pass someone sitting alone on the seawall, casting the line of his or her thoughts into the waves. Most people don't know it, but to sit on a seawall and stare morosely into the ocean is one of life's great pleasures.

A while back, I saw a shiny old man waving a metal detector, looking for his buried youth.

Before that, a man in a Mackintosh coat jogged past me.

I know there's something inherently pretentious about strolling along the shore alone, ruminating—but I do have pretensions.

For one thing, I keep thinking of that scene in *Ulysses* when Stephen Dedalus trudges along Sandymount Strand with his eyes closed, pretending to be blind. He navigates by tapping his ashplant on the broken shells. He wonders if the beach will still be there when he opens his eyes. It is.

An ashplant, by the way, is a walking stick made from a sapling.

I've considered acquiring one for my beach walks, but I'm pretty sure such a literary affectation would not go unremarked upon in Quincy, Massachusetts.

Even James Joyce caught flack for carrying one.

When Joyce was still an aspiring writer, a friend predicted (sarcastically) that his ashplant would someday be the centerpiece of a National Joyce Museum in Dublin.

Joyce didn't appreciate the joke and let the friendship lapse.

Which is a shame really, considering that today there is a James Joyce museum in Dublin, and yes, it does include, among other ephemera, the author's resiny walking stick.

Now that I think of it, a man in a Mackintosh coat jogs through *Ulysses*.

He's an enigmatic figure who haunts the novel. He first shows up at a funeral as the 13th mourner—Death's number, the protagonist thinks with a shudder.

Literary scholars debate his identity.

Is he a ghost?

A character from one of Joyce's earlier works?

Death himself?

Nabokov thought the man in the Mackintosh was Joyce inserting himself into his novel—a Hitchcock cameo—but I don't think so. Joyce always said an author should remain well behind his handiwork, like a remote god paring his fingernails.

Besides, I think Joyce was just perverse.

"I've put in so many enigmas and puzzles that it will keep the professors busy for centuries arguing over what I meant, and that's the only way of ensuring one's immortality," he confided to a friend.

I once got drunk with a Joyce scholar who had spent his life wandering through *Ulysses*. When he heard I was an aspiring writer, he looked doubtfully at me over an amber glass and asked, "Are you sure you're neurotic enough?"

It's something I still worry about to this day.

The sea breeze is picking up. The tide is rising.

I've come upon a nice stretch of empty seawall. I think I'll sit here and stare at the ocean from under my hood.

Maybe I'll count the gulls wheeling over the foaming surf. (Thirteen at a glance.)

Maybe I'll watch for a while as they break open clamshells by dropping them from great heights.

I'll wonder, miserably, if that's what life is doing to me.

It'll be great.

MAY

THE WOOD, THE WEED, THE WAG

SPRING BRINGS A tear to my eye.

Here's how it works:

A few thousand feet above the bovine geometry of Boston, a water molecule combines with a particle of soot released from a power plant in Salem, or perhaps with a spec of black carbon spat from a forest fire in the Berkshires, and then merges with other like-minded molecules within a fast-gliding cumulus to become a cloud droplet, which joins with millions of other cloud droplets, absorbing their pasts—this one ran down Hemingway's glass of beer, this one glistened on a spiderweb in Raleigh's cell, this one wet the sandals of a blind bard in Athens—and grows larger, and heavier, and falls, a raindrop the size of a housefly bearing a history of the world, for approximately six minutes before it lands on the glossy wing of a crow in flight, rolls off, lands on a blade of grass that dips under its new burden, strikes fresh soil and sinks, is displaced by an earthworm, is absorbed by the root hairs of a cherry tree, travels swiftly through xylem vessels and ends up (I'm saving you the indelicate details of germination here) within a pollen grain, where it lingers in the satiny heart of a cherry blossom until, one blustery May morning, it is borne on a breeze and finds at last, as if at the end of a long journey home, the lid of my eye.

RARA AVIS

TODAY IS ONE of those rainy spring days—dripping trees, muddy lawns, earthworms wriggling on wet pavement—that makes me think of the spare, pensive piano music of Erik Satie, a Parisian composer (148 years old this week) who never left his apartment without a bowler hat and one of his hundreds of umbrellas, which he would carry, whenever it rained, rolled-up beneath his yellow corduroy coat lest it get wet.

I've been watching and listening to the birds outside my window.

They're perched like notes on the musical staves of the telephone wires.

I am not, nor have I ever been, a birder—I prefer spotting eccentrics in the foliage of history—but I've always wondered about birdsong, and what it means, and why, when I'm writing at an outdoor cafe and I've had too much espresso, I sometimes suspect the sparrows fluttering beneath the wrought iron tables are talking about me.

The other night, when I couldn't sleep, I sat on my front steps—mild breeze, half-moon sailing—and listened to the dawn chorus. It's an unnerving anthem. So many keyed-up soloists singing as if the world were ending. A black kitten appeared from nowhere, mewled, then sprinted away from my outstretched hand. I watched it disappear between two bushes.

I listened harder, knowing that one of the voices in the chorus would soon be silenced by a set of tiny teeth.

I know it's wise not to ask too much of life, but I would feel cheated if I died before hearing the liquid song of a living nightingale, whose music has been receiving unanimous raves since the invention of the written word.

Well, almost unanimous.

Satie insisted that the bird was overrated. "Not only is its voice not properly placed," he wrote, "but it knows nothing of keys, or pitch, or mode, or measure."

To be fair to the nightingale, neither do I.

Of course, the language of the birds is not a complete mystery. When we listen to birdsong in North America, we're mostly hearing males trying to out-sing each other in competition for a mate.

It certainly worked for Satie.

One night, while he was playing piano at the Auberge du Clou, a cheap nightclub in Montmartre, his music attracted the attention of Suzanne Valadon, a local painter who kept a pet goat in her studio so she could feed it her unsatisfactory drawings. They embarked on an impassioned six-month affair that ended when Satie, consumed by jealousy, pushed Valadon out of her three-story window.

Fortunately, Suzanne Valadon was a true eccentric, which meant that before her life as a painter and an artist's model, she had been a teenage circus acrobat specializing in the trapeze, so she knew just how to land on the paving stones of Rue Cortot and spring to her feet, unscathed, unruffled, and newly single.

IN STONE

ON MEMORIAL DAY, I stooped over my grandfather's grave to rearrange a bunch of geraniums savaged by wild turkeys, removed some flecks of mown grass from the engraved letters of his Korean War plaque, then drove south on Route 24, racing over sun-slick highway, speeding through the shadows of clouds the size of small towns, all the way to Dighton Rock State Park.

Dighton Rock is the gemstone of weird New England.

Borne southward by a sheet of glacial ice about 10,000 years ago, this eleven-foot sandstone boulder came to rest in a riverbed off the shore of Berkley, Massachusetts, where it acquired, sometime in the past couple millennia, a set of mysterious engravings that has become, among a certain subset of historical dilettantes, the subject of wild speculation.

The Puritans assumed the inscriptions were Native American graffiti.

An 18th-century French scholar claimed they were a tableau of Phoenician mythology.

Last century, a Brown University psychologist proposed the now widely accepted theory that a group of Portuguese explorers made the markings before turning around and setting sail for home. (They never made it back.)

Fifty years ago, the rock was hauled on shore and housed in a tiny museum, which, as if to exacerbate the cultural confusion, was modeled on a Greek temple.

The museum was empty when I arrived. The interior was as hushed and dim as a cloister. There were model ships in glass cases, theories on the wall, and a doorway leading to an inner room.

See the rock and decide for yourself, a sign encouraged.

When I entered the sanctum, I found myself in near-darkness. The stone lay behind warped plexiglass. Two glaring spotlights on the rock face made the petroglyphs impossible to discern, let alone decipher.

Disappointed, I wandered back into the antechamber, where I noticed a visitor's book lying open with a blue pen held in its crease.

I began reading.

With each turn of the page, I jumped backward in time approximately three months. While the majority of entries were all business—name and date—many visitors took the opportunity to record their verdict:

"Let there be no doubt this is the work of Native Americans—with some European vandalism."

"Gotta be the Vikings."

"It was God, obviously."

There were confessions of guilt ("I touched the rock, I am sorry"), eruptions of ego ("Today is my birthday"), declarations of despair ("This is a waste of time"), and hopes for future illumination ("I will return with a bigger flashlight").

As I stood there, studying the sundry handwritten entries, I had an epiphany.

I can't tell you who carved Dighton Rock—who waded out there with a stone chisel and labored waist-deep in the lapping current, sometime in the late afternoon when the sun could shine on the boulder's flat westward surface, sometime in late spring when the ice caps of winter had receded, sometime before the onset of summer high-tides and autumnal mud—but I can tell you what Dighton Rock is: a visitor's book.

JUNE

ON HAPPINESS

ALL WINTER, YOU looked forward to summer. You antici-
pated the return of the sun with religious fervor, convinced that
ecstasy and sunlight are the selfsame. But here you are, barefoot
on a green lawn in June, realizing the difficult truth that happiness is not, in fact, photosynthetic.

My people, the Irish, have always been skeptical of happiness. Swift considered it a self-deception; Shaw doubted anyone
could bear it for long ("A lifetime of happiness… would be hell
on earth"); and Joyce, in over 2,000 pages, hardly mentioned it.

Perhaps the island's chronic cloud cover is to blame. It
would explain Samuel Beckett's definition of happiness, perhaps
the saddest ever penned: "We spend our life… trying to bring
together in the same instant a ray of sunshine and a free bench."

In America, you can find no shade from the publicity sur-
rounding the abstract concept of happiness.

Happiness is wanting what you have.

Happiness is learning to dance in the rain.

The aphorisms are everywhere. They descend on you like
inchworms.

We're especially plagued at the moment. It's commencement season, when robed elders indulge in a bit of
self-mythologizing under the guise of advising the next gen-
eration. The theme is always the same—the secret equation of
happiness—and the takeaway is always an empty paradox. This

year, MIT graduates were instructed, or rather commanded, to "Solve the unsolvable!"

It makes me think of Ralph Waldo Emerson, who delivered the commencement address at the Harvard Divinity School in 1838.

(I was recently inside the Divinity Hall Chapel. It's surprisingly small, and it contains the most unforgiving variety of wooden pew I've ever encountered.)

Emerson's speech began well enough: "In this refulgent summer, it has been a luxury to draw the breath of life," he said. "The grass grows, the buds burst, the meadow is spotted with fire and gold in the tint of flowers."

But once he'd covered the weather, Emerson turned his attention to the more controversial topic of incompetent preachers and the decaying church.

He also divulged his secret equation for happiness: Go alone. Don't listen to the bromides, the banalities, the "penny-wisdom." You don't need them. "All men have sublime thoughts," he said. Look inward.

Many Boston clergy regarded the speech as an "incoherent rhapsody" and Emerson himself as "a sort of mad dog." Even his aunt thought he was possibly under the influence of some malevolent demon. He was barred from formal Harvard functions for over thirty years.

It was a blow. Denunciation on such a scale always is, even for an evangelist of self-reliance.

But that October, Emerson's "sunk spirits" suddenly recovered. "[H]ow quick the little wounds of fortune skin over & are forgotten," he wrote in his journal.

He attributed his miraculous change in mood to the cold, crisp air of the autumn nights.

Who doesn't love an autumn night? Aren't we all just counting the days to October, to the wool sweaters and the burning leaves, to when we'll be happy?

NIGHT THOUGHTS

THERE'S AN INSOMNIA native to the beginning of June, when the nights are warm and the air conditioners are still collecting dust in the attic.

I'm sitting up in bed, wishing I were enough of a nonconformist to own a proper diary.

I need a place to put these night thoughts.

I suppose I could take a walk, but something stops me. As Thoreau once wrote, "[M]en are generally still a little afraid of the dark, though the witches are all hung, and Christianity and candles have been introduced."

I've always wondered about Thoreau.

Did he ever get scared out there, alone in the woods at night?

No one ever passed his cabin in the dark—only the night fishermen who came from the village in late spring to cast for pickerel and pouts.

They never had much luck.

According to Thoreau, "They plainly fished much more in the Walden Pond of their own natures, and baited their hooks with darkness."

I've never been able to shake that phrase—*baited their hooks with darkness.*

It always comes back to me when I can't sleep.

When I was a kid, I was made to go night fishing. My father and brother would cast lines off the forearm of Cape Cod while I sat in the cold sand reading by flashlight. Each time I turned a page, some of my light would spill onto the waves and irritate my brother, who swore I was scaring away the fish. One particularly contentious night, he reeled in a striped bass with my exact measurements—height *and* weight—which I took as a direct threat.

I still don't buy my brother's theory that light disperses fish.

Whenever night fishing, Thoreau would kindle a fire at the edge of Walden Pond to attract pout to his line. (He also claimed to drift in his boat and charm perch to the surface by playing the flute.)

For centuries, Mediterranean fisherman used light as bait. They sailed small boats with lamps overhanging the water. The anchovies and sardines, fooled into believing the sun had risen, would squirm into waiting nets.

In the summer of 1939, Picasso encountered these lamp-light fishermen during his long nocturnal walks along the quays of Antibes.

Naturally, he made a painting of it.

It's called *Night Fishing in Antibes*, and it's a hallucinatory, almost hypnotic work.

There's a red spiral inside a full moon, giant moths of pure light, a jade glow pulsing off the seawater.

There's even a joke. One of the men is spearing a sole, a type of flatfish with both eyes on one side of its head.

It's naturally Picassofied.

The painting is on permanent display at The Museum of Modern Art, where it occupies its own wall near the café. I used to stare at it while eating my croissant.

It's my favorite Picasso—which is saying something.

A catalogue of Picasso's complete works was recently reissued. It contains over 16,000 images in 33 volumes and costs $20,000.

Thoreau's cabin cost $28.

Most writers and artists lose sleep over the fear that someday they'll run out of things to say.

Not Picasso.

He was one of those artists who always caught something, who always felt the unmistakable tug as soon as his brush hit the canvas.

"Painting is just a way of keeping a diary," he once said.

Maybe this explains why his pond was always stocked. Have you ever known a diarist to suffer writer's block?

Strangely, Thoreau had the same thought: "Is there any other work for [a poet] but a good journal?" he asked in his journal.

I'm pretty sure Picasso never read any Thoreau.

I'm very sure Thoreau never saw a Picasso.

Thoreau spent ten years carefully editing the manuscript of *Walden*.

Some days Picasso painted four or five canvases.

"Give me a museum and I will fill it," Picasso supposedly said.

I believe it.

Here's why:

In the upper left corner of *Night Fishing in Antibes*, Picasso painted a medieval castle, the Château Grimaldi. The edifice had served as a seafront fortress, then a royal governor's residence, then the town hall of Antibes, then a military barracks. At the time of Picasso's rendering, it was a historical monument.

Today, it is the Musée Picasso.

All Thoreau left behind was a pile of rocks in the woods.

"The youth gets together his materials to build a bridge to the moon…," Thoreau wrote, "and, at length, the middle-aged man concludes to build a woodshed with them."

The full moon is swimming in my window now.

In June, it's called the Strawberry Moon.

Or the Rose Moon.

Or the Long Night Moon.

Tomorrow I'll buy a diary. And a flashlight.

THE LIVELONG JUNE

I WAS THE kind of sensitive child who could get motion sickness just by thinking about the rotation of the Earth. So last Saturday, I half-expected to feel a perceptible tilt toward the sun. It was the summer solstice—the longest day of the year (by one second)—and I spent the entire morning attempting to balance an egg on my kitchen floor. Only later did I realize I had been thinking of the equinox.

I resolved not to tell anyone.

Later, I was drinking on a back porch, watching planes practically skirt the pines on their descent into Logan Airport, when one of my friends stubbed out his cigarette and said, "Hey, check out the sky over there. It's so..."

For a second I thought he was going to say something poetic, but he trailed off like plane exhaust.

In the silence that followed, I recalled those lines by Emily Dickinson: "To see the Summer Sky / Is Poetry, though never in a Book it lie— / True Poems flee."

I resolved not to tell anyone.

Dickinson, who was also a sensitive child, once wrote a poem about the summer solstice, a fleeting day in which the hours slide by as fast as faces on two ship decks "[b]ound to opposing lands."

Dickinson had a preternatural gift for describing the movement of time, perhaps because she couldn't read a clock until she was fifteen. "My father thought he had taught me," she confided to a friend, "but I did not understand & I was afraid to say I did not." So she invented other o'clocks: certain-slant-of-light o'clock, startled-grass o'clock, evening-shadow-holding-its-breath o'clock.

Of course, because the poem is by Dickinson, the summer solstice symbolizes that other lever moment—death. Everything that happens before death is a rehearsal for the afterlife, she writes, a chance to perfect our repartee. That way, the heavenly banquet won't be spoiled by social awkwardness.

I recently tracked mud into Emily Dickinson's parlor. I was distracted by the size and beauty of the house—a spacious Federalist mansion on a hill. I had always imagined Dickinson scribbling quatrains on scraps of paper while scrubbing a fireplace. But now I know the servants would have done that.

While I stood at her bedroom window, watching rain plash off the sill, I wondered why she sent over three hundred letters to her sister-in-law, whose Italian villa-style house stands in full view less than 100 yards away.

Everyone has a theory about why Emily Dickinson withdrew from society. Was it agoraphobia? Anxiety? Epilepsy?

When one of her correspondents asked for a photograph, she demurred, sending instead a written self-portrait: "I... am small, like the wren; and my hair is bold, like the chestnut bur; and my eyes, like the sherry in the glass, that the guest leaves."

I think Dickinson needed, above all else, to control how people saw her. She even stage-managed her funeral in advance, insisting she be carried out the back door (usually reserved for murderers) in a little white casket (usually reserved for children) and buried beneath a tombstone that read *CALLED BACK*.

But you cannot stage-manage conversations. And that's why she feared them more than death. I think she was afraid of trailing off in mid-sentence. I think she was afraid of an awkward silence—the kind a writer can fill with a dash.

So here's to my friend who trailed off on that back porch, the one who lives without dashes or domestics, who doesn't know that Hope is a thing with feathers, who would never leave sherry in the glass—if he ever drank sherry.

JULY

THE SILENT W

BY THE TIME it reached Boston on Thursday night, Hurricane Arthur had mellowed to a tropical storm, which was no comfort to the organizers of the Boston Pops who were forced to cut the fireworks display short, completely scrap Tchaikovsky's "1812 Overture" with its live cannons and church bells (if only they knew their Russian folklore—bells are believed to ward off hurricanes), and evacuate the Esplanade as amber lightning strobed the city and a two-day torrential downpour commenced.

By Saturday, the storm had departed, leaving behind only fitful breezes, some of which can be attributed to sighs of relief from all the Arthurs out there, who narrowly escaped a dramatic rebranding of their name and a permanent association with downed trees and insurance claims.

I've never met an Arthur (I went to public school), but my bookshelves sag with them. Rimbaud, Schopenhauer, Clark, Doyle, Miller. So many authors named Arthur. It's enough to make me believe the theory that our name is our destiny— *nomen est omen*, as the Romans had it. Apparently we feel a sentimental warmth toward our own name and unconsciously steer our lives in whichever direction it points. This explains why a disproportionate number of dentists are named Dennis, and why students whose names begin with C—drawn inexorably toward their cherished initial—have lower grade point averages.

Yet the Arthurs, those academic overachievers, shouldn't breathe too deeply. A storm name is only retired from the list in the case of fatalities and mass destruction. Sooner or later, Arthur's day will come.

And so will William's. (Let's face it—that's where this entry was always headed.)

William is the one name that outstrips Arthur on my bookshelf, though whether this is due to the silent W in writer or to my own implicit egotism, I can't say. There's Yeats, Wordsworth, Faulkner, Blake, Williams, and the guy who famously asked, "What's in a name?"

Supposedly, as a young man, Shakespeare gazed up at Cassiopeia, the W-shaped constellation, and traced his initial among the stars.

It's July, when Cassiopeia begins to rise in the northeastern sky. Every night from now until September, it will cartwheel over Polaris like a slow-motion firework and land upside-down in the hour before dawn, the W capsized into an M.

And this is why I have a better claim on Cassiopeia than Shakespeare. He didn't have a middle name. I do, and it begins with an M.

Of course, I try not to think what my full initials might portend.

Ocean Sounds

Overheard at Nantasket Beach
July 12, 2014

"*There it goes.*"

—A father's detached response to the submersion of his kids' sandcastle. Kids leaning on their shovels, world-weary.

Note: Inevitable—but no one told them.

* * *

"*Bruno, can you believe we still have something left to say to each other?*"

—Retiree in a beach chair. Ragged Red Sox hat. Skin the color of a chewed cigar.

Note: Bruno did not respond, did not even look up. One of his feet lazily buried the other in the sand.

* * *

"*I love matriarchal societies.*"

—Girl with the seahorse tattoo.

Note: Male seahorses gestate and give birth.

* * *

"*You see see see me.*"

—Two-year-old girl in a bumblebee swimsuit buzzing past me in the dunes. Unattended.

Note: Why do some abandoned kids seem to emit a silent alarm, while others give off an unmistakable air of autonomy? This one seemed to know what she was doing.

* * *

"*Not today.*"

—Woman with a grey bun defending her bag of cherries from a swooping seagull.

Note: Sometimes life is uncomplicated.

* * *

"*Stand right here.*"

—Middle-aged daughter down to her last match, trying to light a cigarette, positioning her elderly mother to block the sea breeze.

Note: Mom fanned out her dress and looked down-beach, shaking her head.

* * *

"I feel like Charlotte's gonna capsize us."

—Sister's dire and unheeded warning, which proved prophetic.

Note: Cassandra on an inflatable cabana.

* * *

"There's nothing better than this."

—Unattributed.

Note: Floated out of the crowd like an ownerless swimsuit washing ashore. Might have been an auditory hallucination. Sunstroke?

* * *

"This was a mistake."

—Mother of infant twins. Stroller wheels sunk into the sand.

Note: Unintentionally revealing statement?

* * *

[♫♫ Für Elise ♫♫]

—Ice cream truck broadcasting xylophone Beethoven, casting a melancholy pall on the afternoon.

Note: Depressed teen prodigy behind the wheel? Saving up money for a Stradivarius, one screwball at a time?

* * *

"I don't like to go in the water. I just like to look at it."

—High schooler staying with the stuff while his friends head toward the blue.

Note: The ocean is a paradox: inviting yet forbidding, inhuman yet where we come from, endless yet here we are at the end of it.

* * *

"What do you think he's writing?"

—Guy with neck tattoo. Bike helmet in the sand. Eyeing me from under a camouflage umbrella.

Note: Time to go.

THE PAINTER OF SUNFLOWERS

BETWEEN THE CRUSHING heat of the July sun and the occasional flash flood, it's been a difficult week for people and flowers. We're all feeling a bit withered. Only my neighbor's sunflowers, which bloomed over the weekend, seem to be thriving.

When I spotted these sunflowers, I thought of Vincent Van Gogh, who had already been on my mind. He worshiped sunflowers and painted them compulsively—from life in the summer, from memory in the winter.

A portrait by Paul Gauguin, his friend and rival, shows him in the act. It's called "The Painter of Sunflowers."

Van Gogh hated it. "It's certainly me, but it's me gone mad," he said.

I like its forced perspective, how it looks as if Van Gogh is painting the sunflower itself into existence.

When it comes to Van Gogh and his short life, reality and metaphor are swirled together. This was, after all, a man who nibbled his oil paints like an aspiring synesthete.

It began early, when his mother delivered a stillborn son named Vincent Van Gogh. Our Van Gogh, the replacement child, was born a year later to the day. He was both Vincent and a metaphor for the lost Vincent.

Later, as a painter of blazing pastures in the south of France, he suffered bouts of mania and delirium. Did he stare too long into the sun of his creative passion? Or was it just severe sunstroke?

I think his suicide was a metaphor too—or at least, it was meant to be.

Just a few weeks before Van Gogh shot himself in a wheat field (he'd borrowed a revolver to scare off crows), his brother Theo had announced he was moving to Holland. Theo was the wooden frame to Vincent's stretched canvas. Without Theo, Vincent's financial and emotional survival was at risk.

In the past, whenever someone tried to leave, Van Gogh resorted to self-mutilation. When Gauguin moved out of the Yellow House, he sliced off his left ear with a razor. When a girl he loved skipped town, he held his hand over a candle flame, vowing to keep it there until she returned.

When Van Gogh shot himself in the chest, he missed his heart. It was suppose to be a symbolic act, a metaphor—*this is what you are doing to me, Theo*—and it only became literal as the result of an inept country doctor. At least, that's how I read it.

And this brings me to the reason why Van Gogh has been on my mind. An Italian artist named Diemut Strebe has unveiled a living replica of Van Gogh's left ear—the one he severed—which she recreated using DNA from an envelope Van Gogh sealed in 1883. The ear was grown in Boston with the help of scientists from MIT and Harvard. It's currently on display in a German museum.

Until now, if you hoped to divine the true source of Van Gogh's madness and solve the mystery of his suicide, you had to study the letters and stare at the paintings. How much easier it will be to pluck a red hair from a thick brushstroke and grow another Van Gogh and watch to see how this one kills himself.

Van Gogh was buried in a hilltop cemetery. His coffin was heaped with sunflowers. It was late July. According to one mourner, the sun was unbearable.

AUGUST

HIGH AND DRY

IT'S FRIDAY EVENING, and we're having the kind of sunset that should rightly be seen deliquescing into the canals of Venice, or at the very least glowering over a majestic shipwreck in a Turner painting, and definitely not how I'm seeing it—from the roof of a shopping mall parking garage, framed by light fixtures, marred by swooping pigeons, and undercut by a blazing seam of highway that, at this hour, is alive with centipedal traffic carrying the chosen few to their weekend with an ocean vista while the rest of us are left behind to contemplate our sins.

I suppose the view could be worse.

At least I'm somewhere high.

At least the afternoon clouds have burned off.

At least I'm not colorblind—or at least I don't think I am.

A moment ago, I had the overwhelming urge to write something. After all, the setting sun is to the poet what the spot of blood on the sleeve is to the detective, what the red light above the confessional booth is to the eavesdropper.

But after retrieving a pen and napkin from the recesses of my glove compartment, I found I had nothing to say. I tried to sketch the scene, but how do you render a ball of light with a ballpoint pen? In the end, I resorted to a preschooler's sun—circle, spokes, sunglasses.

I thought of Turner and how in his later years he took up the strange hobby of sun-staring, which he believed would relax his eyes but instead gave him glassblower's cataract. His paintings reddened and yellowed. His dying words were: "The sun is God."

At least I don't have to worry about competing with anyone's dying words.

At least not today.

At least the dew point has dropped.

At least the mosquitos are still asleep.

At least I'm not in a lifeboat at sea.

NIGHT THOUGHTS II

THERE'S AN INSOMNIA native to mid-August, when the nights are as cold and clear as jellyfish and you feel like the only remaining creature alive—or you would, if the neighbor's dog would stop howling at the moon.

A lot of ink has been spilled on the moon this week. Or should I say the *supermoon*.

They claim it won't be this luminous again for twenty years.

I have to admit, it does look spit-shined.

We also just passed, in our calendrical orbit, the 45th anniversary of the first moon landing, which has me thinking not about Neil or Buzz, but about Michael.

Michael Collins was the third crew member on Apollo 11, the one who never actually stepped foot on the lunar surface but stayed aboard the Columbia spacecraft, swiftly circling the moon.

"Not since Adam has any human known such solitude as Mike Collins is experiencing during this 47 minutes of each lunar revolution when he's behind the Moon," Mission Control observed.

Good thing he brought a journal.

During one spell on the dark side, he wrote simply, "I am alone now.... I am it."

Later, while he waited for his colleagues to blast off from the moon and rendezvous with him in orbit, he considered the nightmare possibility that a mechanical failure would leave them stranded.

Armstrong and Aldrin put their odds at 50/50.

Nixon had already prepared their eulogy: "Fate has ordained that the men who went to the Moon to explore in peace will stay on the Moon to rest in peace."

Up in his capsule, Collins imagined the worst. "If they fail to rise from the surface, or crash back into it, I am not going to commit suicide," he wrote. "I am coming home, forthwith, but I will be a marked man for life and I know it."

(For me, these two sentences are proof that man did indeed go to the moon: I find them more convincing than the moon rocks, the ampules of lunar soil, even the recent aerial photos of the Apollo 11 landing site, in which you can make out the discarded Lunar Module like a cigarette burn on the moon's surface.)

Of course, Collins's nightmare proved to be just that—a nightmare.

When they returned to Earth, it was Armstrong and Aldrin who were the marked men, the living memorials who descended into reclusion and alcoholism, respectively.

Meanwhile Collins, who never left a bootprint on lunar dust, sidestepped into a life of peaceful anonymity. Today he lives in Florida and spends his time painting awkward, verdant watercolors of the Everglades.

Until recently Collins refused to sign his paintings, afraid his valuable signature would inflate the price. He didn't want to trade on the accomplishments of his earlier life.

Picasso once refused to sign a painting brought to him for authentication. "If I were to sign it now, I'd be committing forgery. I'd be putting my 1943 signature on a canvas painted in 1922," he said.

After the Apollo mission, Collins felt different from other people—and not just because his time in space made him a fraction of a second younger than his fellow earthlings.

"I have seen the earth eclipsed by the moon," he wrote in his memoir. "Although I have no intention of spending the rest of my life looking backward, I do have this secret, this precious thing, that I will always carry with me."

Most of us will never see the dark side of any moon—but don't we all have a secret, a precious thing, that we carry inside? A thing that makes us strange and lonely and ourselves?

A Chess Problem

THIS MORNING I got up early and sat on my back porch and worked my way through a stack of week-old newspapers.

I was testing a pet theory.

People claim the full moon triggers a collective lunacy, flooding emergency rooms and holding cells. If that's true, just imagine what the supermoon unleashed last weekend.

I rifled through the papers, skimming over the usual sprees. At last I found something out of the ordinary: a report of the 41st Chess Olympiad in Tromsø, Norway.

The tournament got off to an uneventful start, but right around the time the supermoon waxed, things got weird.

A player from Uzbekistan was found dead in his hotel room. Then the women's team from Burundi vanished after round five (according to Norwegian officials, they're still unaccounted for). And during his final match, a member of the Seychelles team collapsed from a heart attack. He was rushed to the hospital, where he was pronounced dead.

If this last incident sounds somehow familiar to you, that's just because life has once again lifted a plot from Agatha Christie.

In her short story "A Chess Problem," a grandmaster suffers a heart attack in the middle of a game when his metallic white bishop touches a surreptitiously electrified board.

Agatha Christie was a decent chess player.

Most mystery novelists are.

Poets are lousy at chess, which is surprising given the parallels (the perpetual starting over, the inevitable madness), though of course poetry is played not in a smoky backroom with fellow hollow-eyed obsessives but alone, the right hand against the left, with pieces that can breed and recombine on an endless board of overlapping squares.

The most successful game of chess ever played by a poet took place at the White Horse Tavern in the late 1940s, when Dylan Thomas—who would later die after being served 18 whiskies at the bar—vomited on the board, blasting the pieces onto his opponent's lap.

Which was, I suppose, a kind of endgame.

I once ducked into the White Horse Tavern to escape an afternoon downpour. I elbowed my way through the shrieking crowd and asked the bartender for 18 whiskies, which is something she must have heard before, since, without looking up, she replied, "Only if you promise to die."

Checkmate.

I keep thinking of that member of the Seychelles team, and how his mid-game demise was recorded by tournament officials as a loss, and how his individual ranking will take a posthumous tumble.

Chess is a cold, ruthless amusement.

Take the case of Magnus Carlsen, the 23-year-old Norwegian grandmaster and current World Champion, whose shocking defeat at the Olympiad was drowned out by the deaths and disappearances.

Was it exhaustion?

Was it the airlessness of a room in which 650 chess matches were being played simultaneously?

Was it the fact that the Prime Minister of Norway made his opening move in what must be the international equivalent of throwing out the first pitch?

After the game, Carlsen told reporters that his creativity had abandoned him. He just felt empty.

I'm supposed to describe the weather this morning. I'm supposed to think of an original way to describe the blue sky and the white clouds.

I found a single fallen acorn on the porch. I should probably make something of that.

But I'm not in the mood to describe anything right now.

I just feel empty.

And I don't care if my ranking goes down.

It's like Dylan Thomas said: "Poetry is not the most important thing in life. I'd much rather lie in a hot bath reading Agatha Christie."

SEPTEMBER

THE GATSBY HOUSE

PERSONALLY, I DON'T understand the confusion.

The end of summer falls clearly and cleanly on the folded crease between the last day of August and the first day of September.

No one understood this better than F. Scott Fitzgerald. *The Great Gatsby* climaxes on the last sweltering afternoon of August; the next morning, the neighborhood kids are sneaking through Nick Carraway's backyard to steal a glimpse of Gatsby floating face down in his pool like a dead leaf.

When I was fourteen and under the spell of Fitzgerald's masterpiece, I nicknamed a mansion in my neighborhood—the only mansion in my neighborhood—the Gatsby house. I would fly past it on my bike and wonder when my name would be on the deed.

One summer afternoon, my friends and I snuck into the backyard. We dove into the cerulean swimming pool, then sunk all the patio furniture. I remember the owner—an old man in owl glasses—appearing at the edge of the pool with his arms spread wide, saying, "You could have just asked."

Sometimes, when I think of all the term papers written on *The Great Gatsby*—those desperate attempts to decipher the symbolic significance of that notorious green light—I imagine Fitzgerald appearing at the edge of the page with his arms spread wide, saying, "You could have just asked."

When *The Great Gatsby* was first published, critics dismissed it as "clever and brilliantly surfaced but not the work of a wise and mature novelist." One reviewer forecast, "This is a book for the season only."

Fitzgerald was crushed.

How could he have predicted that his novel would become a rite of passage for future high schoolers on par with Prom?

(I must have read the book three or four times in high school before I noticed the naked women on its iconic cover—their bodies swim in the irises of the disembodied face.)

Like all great works of literature, *The Great Gatsby* has a reflective quality. It changes as you change. When I read the novel this summer, I naturally saw it as a wistful commentary on turning thirty.

I also saw it as a seasonal dialectic. On the one hand you have Gatsby, the master of midsummer revels, a man whose very name sounds like a species of short-lived summer fly; on the other hand you have Nick, the solemn narrator, an East Coast transplant who can't seem to shake the December evenings of his Middle West youth. All those streetlamps and sleigh bells and shadows of holly wreaths on snow—is it any wonder that when the party crowd disperses, Nick sticks around for Gatsby's cold and rain-soaked funeral?

I recently learned a curious piece of family history.

It turns out that my great-grandmother Ann Morrissey lived for years in my Gatsby house, serving as a cook and companion to the wealthy widow who resided there. Perhaps, given the circumstances, she might have found the house willed to her—those things do happen. But late one summer night, Ann thought she heard someone trying to break in (probably some local kids). She moved out the next day.

I spent my childhood pedaling and pining for the brick mansion, not understanding that my chance had already come and gone.

"His dream must have seemed so close that he could hardly fail to grasp it," Nick says of Gatsby. "He did not know that it was already behind him, somewhere back in that vast obscurity."

I don't know what *The Great Gatsby* is really about. Or what the green light signifies. All I know is that the season's cigarette has burned down to its holder.

The summer is over, and I haven't been to any good parties.

A Certain Unwholesome Sultriness

THE FIRST WEEK of September brought forth a heat so biblical that we New Englanders wandered around mopping sweat from our eyes and confessing to uncommitted murders. Finally, a long-forecast storm arrived on Saturday evening and lit blue matches in the sky. Thunder rumbled like the apneic snores of a sleeping God.

That metaphor—thunder as the awful voice of God—comes straight from the Puritans. I always think of them around this time of year when we're in the throes of late-summer mugginess. I imagine them bundled up in their corsets and petticoats and capes and linen caps, and I wonder how they clung to sanity.

I suppose they had their faith.

Yet how much consolation did they find in their Calvinist reading of the world?

According to their belief in predestination, a few select souls will spend the afterlife in unimaginable seraphic bliss, while the rest are damned to hell. Here's the rub: just who is saved and who is damned is fixed before birth, before time began, in fact. All that is left to do is to worry.

To me, it seems predestined that the Puritans should have ended up in New England. Is there a better climate on Earth for worrying about the state of your soul? If you can't feel God's grace, just wait five minutes.

Puritan sermons were, of course, full of weather. From high pulpits, preachers bellowed about hellfire humidity and clarifying frosts.

In my life, I've never delivered a single sermon.

Here goes.

In August 1637, just a few miles from where I live, a woman named Anne Needham Hett was in such distress over her spiritual estate that she threw her newborn daughter into a well. Now I am sure I shall be damned for I have drowned my child, she announced.

Someone rushed to the well and pulled the girl out in time.

Five years later, in the same state of mind, Anne stripped her three-year-old son naked and threw him into the deepest section of the creek behind her house.

Someone passing by dove in and pulled the boy out in time.

This was the last straw. Anne was whipped and excommunicated.

When she was allowed back into the fold a year later, it was only because she had reconciled herself to abiding uncertainty.

She had to live the rest of her life not knowing what weather awaited her after death.

Of one thing, however, she could be certain: her children were definitely among the saved.

SHADOWPLAY

WHEN I BEGAN this weather journal, I made a solemn promise to myself that no matter what happened (meteorologically or biographically), I would never under any circumstances use the word "dapple"—and so far, I've been as good as my word.

But now that the light of mid-September has leaked from its carton, I'm beginning to feel the strain.

For example, I want to describe the scene in front of me.

I'm sitting on a bench. Under a tree. Facing water.

I sometimes come here on Sunday mornings to eat a blueberry bagel and think about my life while the pond throws stones at me.

Have you ever encountered a literary bench that wasn't sun-*****ed?

It's not that I find the word too effete. The poet Gerard Manley Hopkins used it ("Glory be to God for dappled things—"), and just look at his middle name.

But I drew a line in the sun-*****ed sand and I won't cross it.

What's a writing style if not a refusal to use certain words, even under the duress of deadlines and seasonal demands?

The clouds are casting patterns of calico shadow over the surface of the parking lot.

The light coming off the water is cool and yellow, as if exhaled from an open refrigerator.

There's a swan trailing bolts of light like an electric eel.

In the end, all we have are our scruples—and our thesaurus.

Smoke and Mildness

It's THE POINTY end of September, when gazebos should be cages for wet leaves and pool covers should be billowing like black shrouds.

But instead we're having an Indian summer.

The expression "Indian summer" was most likely coined by early New England settlers, for whom an unexpected flush of autumnal warmth carried the threat of a late-season assault by Native Americans.

As the casual appropriation of Native American culture increasingly captures the attention of the national media, I can't help but wonder if "Indian summer" is due for rebranding.

(I grew up in a town with a Native American mascot, where my own historical consciousness was helped along by occasionally stepping barefoot on an arrowhead.)

Surprisingly, America is not the only country with a controversial name for the season. In Bulgaria they call the phenomenon "Gypsy Christmas"; in other European countries they dub it "Summer of Crones." Both appellations are inspired, supposedly, by the mid-autumn proliferation of flying spiders, whose gossamer threads recall the grey hair of old women suspected of witchcraft.

"Indian summer" first appeared in print in the letter of a French immigrant farmer, who defined the season as "a short Interval of Smoke and Mildness" before the arrival of a "voluminous Coat of snow." By the 19th century, the term was widespread.

I remember once reading that the artist and naturalist John James Audubon lived for Indian summer. He called it "that happy season of unrivalled loveliness and serenity."

A lot of people hate John James Audubon.

They consider him an avian serial killer whose impeccable brushwork cannot excuse his crimes against nature. It's true he killed and posed his winged subjects with little remorse—but perhaps life had hardened his heart. As a young man, when his flour mill failed and a family of Kentucky rats ate his entire collection of over 200 drawings, he clawed his way out of debt by painting deathbed portraits.

"Unfortunately naturalists are obliged to eat and have some sort of garb," he remarked in his journal.

Audubon became renowned for his ability to generate the illusion of life with a piece of black chalk. Like a doctor or priest, he was summoned at all hours to sketch people as they faded from this world. A clergyman from Louisville even had his dead child disinterred for an Audubon portrait.

I'm not sure if moonlighting at deathbeds took a toll on Audubon. He never seemed to mention it in his journal.

Instead, he wrote about the weather, especially "that delightful and peculiarly American autumnal season called the Indian summer." In Audubon's eyes, it was the most rich and glowing time of year, more pure even than the summer itself.

Many people—myself included—think very highly of Indian summer, tinged as it is with the coming of winter. But only someone steeped in death and simulacrum could prefer a mock season to the real thing.

Only John James Audubon could prefer the summer dead and stuffed.

OCTOBER

THE FIRST DRAFT OF AN EARLY FALL

IT WAS A blurry week of rain and mist and moths. Of red leaves strewn like tickets to a rained-out concert. Seven palindromic days of sogginess and lethargy when all one could do was stare out a rain-streaked window and write rhyming couplets in the condensation.

Autumn has always been poets' weather.

There's at least one famous poet who admits she can only write in the fall, when a certain gnawing chill enters her knuckles. (This same poet once told me that her cat, William, writes most of her best poems.)

Among the Romantics, you weren't cool unless you had at least a quatrain on the wanton grandeur of the season. Keats had his "season of mists," Byron his "mellow autumn," Wordsworth his "pensive beauty," and Clare his "fitful gust."

While they were all swimming in Shakespeare's inkwell, only the pastoral poet John Clare went so far as to claim authorship of Shakespeare's work.

"I'm John Clare now," he told an editor who visited him in Northampton General Lunatic Asylum. "I was Byron and Shakespeare formerly. At different times, you know, I'm different people—that is, the same person with different names."

While Clare's doctor blamed his madness on "years of poetical prosing," Clare himself blamed the autumn, a season that never failed to swaddle him in a "stupor of chilling indisposition."

It's an old idea—a Greek idea—that souls travel, that they pass through terrestrial, aquatic and winged forms, that in due course some of them sit upright and hold a quill, that among these are a few poets who return century after century to defy the right margin.

I don't believe in literary reincarnation, of course.

So what if the definitive dissertation on metempsychosis in English romantic poetry was written in the late 1940s by one Wilfred Dowden?

Still, the idea was on my mind this week when I met my oldest friend's newborn son. He was squirming in a mechanical swing, dressed in a sock, still scowling from his amphibious assault on the world. (No matter what ill-considered piercings or lizard sleeve tattoos we acquire over the years, we never outdo that first metamorphosis from water creature to land animal.)

It occurred to me that this child, born one week ago, has never seen the sun. For him, the rain has always been falling, the wind always howling. Just imagine the romantic poem he could write.

If only his hands weren't mittened and he had the fine motor skills to grip a pen.

If only he had some words to work with rather than the wet leaves that stir and scatter in sudden gusts behind his eyes.

At one point, he opened his pursed mouth and I thought maybe, if he were Milton or Dante returned, some verse might emerge.

But it was just milk spittle.

It was definitely not poetry.

I suppose it might have been art. It's hard to tell these days.

THE SEASON OF THE SOUL

I LOVE TO take long Sunday morning walks in October when the wind is crisp and the leaves are tumbling down and every twenty feet or so you have to step over the viscera of a shattered pumpkin.

This morning I was almost run over. I was distracted by a dozen crows screaming in an oak tree. It might have been a crow funeral (they do that).

Anyway, an ultramarine minivan blew through a stop sign (they do that) and missed my foot by a foot.

Afterward, I spent a long time fiddling with my iPod, trying to find a song for the occasion of not being flattened. I thought of Nietzsche, who preferred his music "cheerful and profound, like an October afternoon."

Nietzsche had an autumn problem. For ten years he wandered Europe like a hypochondriac Goldilocks looking for a warm, but not humid, autumnal climate. He finally settled on Turin, whose impeccable grid of paved streets allowed him to take walks despite his failing eyesight.

"Wonderful clarity," he wrote upon arriving in Turin, "autumn colors, an exquisite sense of well-being emanating from all things."

Of course, it was on one of these morning walks that Nietzsche encountered a broken-down carthorse being whipped.

He flung his arms around the animal, sobbed violently, and never regained his sanity.

I didn't see anything this morning to make me lose my sanity. Just some roses on their deathbeds. Just the sun, low in the sky, sliding its meager warmth like a final offer face down across a table.

But I do keep thinking of that close call, and how my ancestors, every last forefather and foremother, survived without exception to bear children, and how those children in turn survived to bear children—an unbroken chain of human beings who never ate the wrong berry, who never missed the snake in the grass, who never misjudged the strength of a branch or their own strength in the waves, who were never the friend drowned in the creek but always the friend who ran home dripping to tell about it, who were never the mourned, always the mourning, forever, all the way back, pin balanced on pin, the ultimate winning streak, the inconceivable, astonishing luck of it.

A TEMPEST AND A TEAPOT

I HAVE DECIDED, in solidarity with those New Englanders who lost power during the midweek nor'easter, to handwrite this entry, and, if that lends a flavor of impermanence to my words, just think of all the diplomas and wedding photos that took a basement bath this week (overnight downpours, leaf-filled drains) and reflect on the deep puddles of standing water that even this morning are hosting regattas for the paper sailboats of some poor bastard's mail.

I haven't experienced this kind of flooding since the fall of 2007, when I used to eat sushi for lunch everyday in MIT's Stata Center.

A yellow and white aluminum scrapheap of a building, the Stata Center was designed by Frank Gehry to look like "a party of drunken robots got together to celebrate." (I've always considered it a cubist omelet.)

When the $300 million contraption began to leak and MIT filed suit, the architect responded by announcing to a crowd, "My name's Frank Gehry, and my buildings don't leak." I couldn't help but admire the sheer audacity of the man, even as I avoided brimming buckets and ducked under caution tape.

A lot of people hate Frank Gehry.

To them, he's like a storm that rolls into a city, deposits a monstrosity, then dissipates.

What seems to gall them the most is his method.

Each of his buildings is born from a whimsical sketch, wispy as a signature, which he proceeds to turn into glass and steel.

In a way, his buildings are handwritten—and that troubles the sort of people who are afraid to get their socks wet.

"Life is chaotic, dangerous, and surprising," he once said. "Buildings should reflect that."

I tend to agree with Gehry, but even I have my limits.

"I did a teapot and nobody bought it," he complained in a recent interview.

Oh Frank, I wonder why?

NOVEMBER

SILVER ASLANT

THIS MORNING I planned to write about the smoldering festival of Samhain, when Celtic druids would light leggy bonfires on hilltops to stave off the growing darkness of winter, and then I planned to speculate on what bloody pagan rites we might enact to stave off the growing darkness of daylight saving time, a tradition (abolished in Russia this week with a flick of Putin's pen) that I despise, not simply because the early twilight plays havoc with our circadian rhythms, but because the very concept represents a hubristic human meddling in the oceanic mystos of time.

I was going to write about all this, but then the rain turned to snow.

I saw it happen through the café window. The cold drizzle was suddenly full of white feathers.

It made me think of Howard Nemerov, who claimed that the difference between prose and poetry was the difference between rain and snow (one falls, one flies).

I'm not sure I agree with Nemerov.

Maybe poetry is just prose dropped from a loftier height, the words crystalizing on the way down. Or maybe it's the other way around. I try not to brood too much over such things.

I don't want to end up like Yury Nikitkin.

Yury Nikitkin was a 66-year-old Russian man who loved literature. On a snowy evening last January, he invited an old friend to his home. The two men began draining shots of vodka. Before long, they were in a heated argument over which literary genre was more important—poetry or prose. While Nikitkin contended that prose was the real literature, his guest insisted it was poetry. The guest settled the dispute by plunging a knife into Nikitkin's chest, then fleeing to a nearby village (one falls, one flies).

The poetry lover was caught and, earlier this week, sentenced to eight years in a penal colony.

What I find most disturbing about this literary murder is the fact that Yury Nikitkin loved poetry too. He was well-known in his small town as an unemployed eccentric who would stop people in the snow-powdered streets to recite the verses he'd committed to memory.

If I were sitting in a dusky bar right now, I would down a shot of vodka in Yury Nikitkin's memory.

But I'm in a café—and that's probably for the best. When considering the relative merits of prose and poetry, one should stick to coffee.

PAPER ALLEGORIES

THE NIGHTS WERE cold this week, and so were the days; the sun, when it appeared, flashed like a coin at the bottom of a well, and the rain fell whenever it felt like it. It was really and truly November, though I couldn't quite accept it. I walked down my street kicking acorns and attempting to reattach fallen leaves.

I kept thinking of the opening of *Moby-Dick*, when Ishmael declares it a damp, drizzly November in his soul.

I have never properly read *Moby-Dick*—it is the white whale of my reading life, the pale rippling shadow that glides under the surface of American literature and will someday swallow me.

All I really know of Melville's novel is that the albino sperm whale of the title is a symbol for, among other things, an unknowable God.

(Maybe that's why the book is filed, in my mind, next to the theory that the Earth stands on the back of a turtle, which stands on the back of another turtle, and that it's turtles all the way down.)

When *Moby-Dick* was published, most critics considered the book unfathomable trash. Melville was not surprised. "Not one man in five cycles, who is wise, will expect appreciative recognition from his fellows," he wrote. He had long ago resigned himself to a career of being misunderstood.

That is, until he met Nathaniel Hawthorne.

The two were introduced on a hike in the Berkshires and hit it off. Within weeks Melville purchased a farmhouse down the road from his new friend and literary mentor. They exchanged frequent letters. When Hawthorne praised *Moby-Dick* (as I imagine you must praise a novel that is dedicated to you), Melville was beyond touched.

On November 17, 1851, he took up his pen and wrote perhaps the most zealous thank-you letter ever composed in English.

"A sense of unspeakable security is in me this moment, on account of your having understood the book," he wrote to his neighbor. "Your heart beat[s] in my ribs and mine in yours." Then Melville, whose father had died from pneumonia after a winter ride in an open horse carriage, paid Hawthorne the most deeply felt compliment his life history could offer. "Ah! it's a long stage," he wrote of life, "and no inn in sight, and night coming, and the body cold. But with you for a passenger, I am content and can be happy."

Perhaps Melville came on too strong. In a postscript, he promised to establish a paper mill at one end of his house—that way he would have an endless ribbon of foolscap rolling across his desk, upon which he would write "a thousand—a million—a billion thoughts," all in the form of a letter to Hawthorne.

Hawthorne promptly moved away.

I hate to think of Melville treading in the wake of this rejection, especially when *Moby-Dick* proved a critical and commercial failure. His next book, *Pierre*, fared even worse;

one newspaper's review bore the headline "Herman Melville Crazy"—a sentiment shared by his in-laws, who exhorted his wife Lizzie to leave him, even offering to stage her fake kidnapping. When Lizzie decided to stay, the family used their influence to secure Melville a position as a Customs Inspector at the New York docks, which he described as worse than driving geese. He held the post for 19 years, all the while hoping for an autumnal masterpiece that never quite materialized.

Strangely, I don't believe Melville regretted that November letter. He knew it sounded desperate and mad—like a "flame in the mouth." But he would have written it again. And again. And again.

"In me divine magnanimities are spontaneous and instantaneous—catch them while you can."

If there's an allegory to be found in Melville's life, it tells us this: spread your divine magnanimities while you can, for tomorrow could be a November in your soul, and a November can last twenty years.

You never know.

It could be Novembers all the way down.

FROST RECIDIVOUS

THIS WEEK, AS New England endured a senseless pre-winter cold snap, I drove (against all animal instinct) north, deep into what I call Frost country, that leafy swathe of Vermont and New Hampshire where the poet spent his life pinballing between picturesque farmhouses—though I imagine, after a week like this, even Robert Frost, the poet laureate of visible breath, would have torched his rustic cabin and headed for the Florida coast, retiring from the pen and paper racket to spend his last days dabbling in the trade of rare orchids.

As I was the first member of the bachelor party to arrive at the rental house, which was perched on a rocky hillside overlooking a frothing Atlantic bay, the gentle and unblinking owner gave me a thorough tour, pointing out various features of the original home he had lovingly restored.

I felt sick to my stomach thinking of the potential destruction that lay ahead.

I remembered the news stories from a few years ago, when the local teens of Middlebury, Vermont held a midwinter bacchanal in Frost's final farmhouse. For desecrating the historic home, they were sentenced to mandatory poetry classes.

The case still bothers me.

I hate the way the prosecutor wielded Frost's poetry like a switch from a birch tree, especially considering how much the poet detested formal education. Frost was against learning poetry in a classroom: he thought we should "settle down like a revolving dog and make ourselves at home among the poems, completely at our ease as to how they should be taken."

The prosecutor clearly subscribed to the image of Frost as Old Man Winter, as a folksy sage who dropped chestnuts of wisdom and exhaled bracing gusts of common sense. He believed that forcing the vandals to read Frost's poetry would be like standing them by an open window in winter—it would make them a little more serious about their lives.

Frost had a son named Carol, a failed farmer and poet who, at the age of thirty-eight, committed suicide with a deer-hunting rifle. After the tragedy, Frost penned a haunting letter. "[Carol] thought too much," he wrote. "I couldn't make him ease up on himself and take life and farming off-hand."

Later in the same letter, Frost concedes just how much of his life he had spent, both as a father and as a roving lecturer, telling other people how to live. His son's death humbled him. "I acknowledge myself disqualified from giving counsel," he wrote.

To me, the teenage trespassers did not receive poetic justice, as every headline declared. I would have sentenced them to clean up their mess and left them to discover Frost's poetry as adults.

After all, haven't we all broken into our fair share of Frost's houses, and rocked ourselves in his iambic rocking chair, and got a little drunk on his mulled wisdom?

There's not much to say about my weekend in Frost country.

Yes, funny things occurred—but as Frost once said, to appreciate the jokes you made when you were drunk, you have to get drunk again.

What happened will have to stay up north with the picturesque farmhouses, and the ice-blue skies, and the shining russet leaves, and the security deposit.

DECEMBER

LEFTOVERS

ON A WALK one morning not long after Thanksgiving, I was confronted by a wild turkey. It stepped out from behind a telephone pole and began pacing the sidewalk. I stood there for a long time, waiting for it to move on or ask me a riddle. Eventually, I took an alternate route.

I got away lucky.

This week the Greater Boston area saw an unprecedented outbreak of turkey attacks. Joggers were chased. Mailmen were mauled. Crossing guards were bullied.

"There was like six or seven of them," a Brookline woman told a local news station, "and as I went around the mailbox they went around and they started chasing me into the street and I screamed for help."

Across the region, town councils are holding emergency meetings for people to share their stories.

"I can't believe we're living this way," said a frustrated citizen who recently got a turkey in the face.

Everyone is demanding to know how we got here.

By the 1840s, wild turkeys had been hunted to the brink of extinction in Massachusetts. The last flock held out on the rugged peak of Mount Tom, its numbers dwindling until finally, in the winter of 1851, a single turkey was left.

It was shot and mounted.

For a century, the residents of Massachusetts enjoyed simple and untroubled lives.

Then, in a stunning act of hubris, state wildlife officials released 37 wild turkeys into the hills of Western Massachusetts. I think they were hoping for a few flocks roosting on remote peaks. Today 30,000 turkeys are strutting statewide, targeting children and the elderly.

Fortunately, the Humane Society has released new recommendations for fending off turkey attacks:

Hurl tennis balls.

Brandish an open umbrella.

Spray a hose.

Establish dominance and do not, under any circumstances, run.

Find a strategy now, they urge, because things will only get worse in February. That's when mating season begins.

MORNING THOUGHTS

IT'S A MID-MORNING in mid-December, and the snow is already falling like shredded paperwork, and I'm already at the bar, stirring the celery in my second Bloody Mary.

I'm still thawing out from the walk here. The temperature outside is cryogenic. On the street I encountered no life forms aside from a pack of mechanical reindeer grazing on my neighbor's lawn.

I call this Shackleton weather, when you reach your destination with a beard of icicles and smelling of seal meat.

I once tried to read *South*, Ernest Shackleton's account of his disastrous 1914 mission to stroll across Antarctica. I found it incredibly dull—except for one passage. When his ship was crushed in ice floes, Shackleton made a treacherous hike across South Georgia Island to reach a whaling station. He took with him his two most trusted crew members.

Later, he wrote:

"I know that during that long and racking march of 36 hours over the unnamed mountains and glaciers of South Georgia, it seemed to me often that we were four, not three. I said nothing to my companions on the point, but afterwards Worsley said to me, 'Boss, I had a curious feeling on the march that there was another person with us.' Crean confessed to the same idea."

I've always been fascinated by the "Third Man syndrome," as it's called—the phenomenon wherein explorers and adventurers, on the brink of death, encounter a ghostly presence who encourages them to keep going.

Naturally there's a debate:

Is the Third Man simply a figment of the burned-out brain, a delusion brought on by dehydration and hypoxia?

Or is it something more?

According to one theory, the Third Man is the neurological answer to extreme loneliness.

Take Charles Lindbergh, who was not the first man to fly nonstop across the foaming Atlantic, but rather the first one to do it alone. His achievement was one of solitude and sleep deprivation. He stayed awake for over 55 hours, dodging fog banks and skirting thunderheads. He even skimmed the ocean surface, hoping the salt spray on his face would keep him conscious.

About halfway through his journey, Lindbergh suddenly realized he was not alone in the plane. While staring at the instruments, he felt the fuselage behind him crowd with "ghostly presences." One by one, these phantoms pressed themselves to his ear and spoke above the engine's noise. They advised him on his flight, pointed out flaws in his navigation, and reassured him with "messages of importance unattainable in ordinary life."

Hours later, Lindbergh landed in a floodlit airfield where a mob of 150,000 Parisians hauled him from his monoplane and tossed him around like a living souvenir.

The phantoms were gone, and he never saw them again. Perhaps he never needed to. Within a year, he met and married Anne Morrow, who became his copilot and navigator.

It makes sense that the Third Man is simply a projected companion, an oasis for the lonely. But one thing puzzles me. Why did Lindbergh keep his encounter secret for three decades? And why was Shackleton so reluctant to discuss his experience?

Both men proudly owned up to their other mid-journey mirages. Lindbergh reported seeing fog islands, while Shackleton described levitating icebergs and golden Oriental cities shimmering on clifftops.

Yet when it came to the Third Man, they both clammed up.

"There are some things which never can be spoken of," Shackleton told a friend. "Almost to hint about them comes perilously near to sacrilege."

Which brings us to the religious explanation. What if these Third Men are the real deal? The *angelus custos*? The divine escorts whose slick wings quiver in the spoon like empyrean of peripheral vision?

But I don't go in for that sort of thing.

After all, here I am on a Sunday morning, stooped before rows of gleaming liquor bottles arrayed in tiers like a pipe organ, playing the only hymn I know.

The snow has stopped falling, at least for the moment.

The window is a brick of pearl.

I keep catching my reflection in the bar mirror.

I think I'll order a third Bloody Mary—just for a little company.

WINTER BLOOM

EACH YEAR, IN the frosty handful of days between Christmas and New Year's, something strange happens in my corner of New England. The decorative mangers, which my neighbors prop in their rose gardens and spotlight from nearby trees, are suddenly bereft of their bargain store baby dolls. The straw remains, but the dolls are simply gone—stolen or resurrected.

Sometimes they're found weeks later dangling from a basketball net or half-buried in a snowbank. Are they the victim of roving teens offended by a vestige of childhood? A coyote looking for a new chew toy?

Perhaps it's just a law of the universe that dolls go missing.

In recent years, my grandmother has taken a precautionary measure. She loops a thin metal wire around the doll's plastic ankle and tethers it to the manger. So far, it's worked.

The whole thing reminds me of the story of Franz Kafka and the doll.

One autumn day, while walking through a small neighborhood park, Kafka and his lover, Dora Diamant, came upon a little girl in tears. She had lost her doll. "Your doll has simply gone on a journey," Kafka told her. "I know this because she's written me a letter." The girl was dubious. "Have you got it on you?" "No, I left it at home by mistake, but I'll bring it with me tomorrow." Kafka rushed home and began to write in the same state of feverish intensity that always consumed him when he composed fiction. Every day for the next three weeks, he returned to the park with a new letter, which he read aloud to the little girl. In each missive, the doll told of her adventures. She grew up, went to school, met people. Soon the little girl was so absorbed by the tale that she forgot about her toy. In the end, Kafka brought the storyline to its natural conclusion—an engagement, a wedding, a house in the country. "You yourself will understand," wrote the doll, "we must give up seeing each other."

This anecdote is difficult to swallow.

An author penning a serialized fantasy to cheer up a tearful child in a park sounds more like J. M. Barrie than Franz Kafka— that tall, dark-eyed, emaciated figure from whose spiky shadow children surely fled.

In recent years, Kafka scholars have tried desperately to find the little girl, who would be in her nineties today, in the hope of authenticating the story. They have published articles in major newspapers with headlines such as "Who Met Kafka in the Park?"

Yet the little girl has never been found. Did she leave home and travel the world like her doll? Was she Jewish and killed in the Holocaust?

Perhaps it's just a law of the universe that people go missing.

What I love most about the story is how Kafka, for all his radical generosity, did not simply buy the little girl a new doll. That would have made for a parable of consolation; that would have implied that the universe is governed by a kind of Newtonian conservation of dolls. Instead, Kafka gave her a tale so captivating that she completely forgot her missing toy, an exchange that suggests physical objects and stories are—as Einstein discovered of mass and energy—different forms of the same thing.

But maybe I'm overthinking the doll story.

Incidentally, it's possible that Kafka and Einstein met.

They were both living in Prague in the winter of 1912, and according to legend the physicist serenaded the brooding writer with his violin at a literary salon.

When I spent a snowy December week in Prague reading and rereading *The Metamorphosis*, I saw a plaque in Old Town Square commemorating the meeting. Next door they were selling Franz Kafka finger puppets.

It was a strange time for Einstein, that winter he lived in Prague. He spent long afternoons in his office at the Institute of Theoretical Physics grappling with the dual nature of light and staring out the window at a shady park across the street.

Eventually he noticed something odd. Every morning the park filled up with women—only women—and every afternoon with men—only men. Some wandered deep in thought while others clustered in groups and engaged in heated discussions.

When Einstein finally asked, he learned that the park belonged to an insane asylum. "Those are the madmen who do not occupy themselves with the quantum theory," he remarked to a friend.

It would require a complex equation, beset with countless variables and hinging on as yet undivined human calculus, to explain why certain people occupy the insane asylum and others the Institute of Theoretical Physics.

Or why certain people are remembered long after their death (J. M. Barrie called them "December roses") while the rest of us are buried and forgotten.

Kafka very nearly missed out on being a December rose. He burned approximately 90 percent of what he wrote during his lifetime, and before dying of tuberculosis at age 41, he left his remaining oeuvre in the hands of a friend with one simple instruction: Burn everything. Fortunately, he trusted the wrong friend.

Kafka's younger brothers, Georg and Heinrich, died in infancy.

His favorite sister, Ottla, was murdered in the crematoriums of Auschwitz.

Dora succumbed to kidney failure and was laid to rest in an unmarked grave in east London.

There's nothing you can do to guarantee you will bloom a December rose.

If you want to be remembered, my only advice is this: find a genius, loop a thin metal wire around his or her ankle, and hold on tight.

OUTRO

DEAR READER,

It's January 1st, and it's absurdly cold. The bitter salt wind on my face is like Novocain wearing off.

I've brought my hangover to the ocean, that church for the churchless, that substitute for pistol and ball.

There are plenty of joggers making the first and last strides of their New Year's resolutions, but I didn't come here to run. I came here to walk along the water and take notes as I stare down at the sea-wrack Rorschach. So far I've spotted a shattered shell (severed ear), a strand of seaweed (mermaid bra), and a washed-up horseshoe crab (the death mask of a great poet).

Is that what New England weather is to us?

An inkblot?

Maybe that's why we keep talking about it—for the simple pleasure of feeling our inner and outer worlds, however briefly and superficially, overlap.

There's a seam of sea foam running the length of the beach. I scoop some up in my hands.

Sophocles said that love is like ice in the hands of children.

I have no idea what he meant.

It's been a joy to wrestle for the past year with the god of New England weather, that artful trickster, but I'm tired now.

I think I'll buy one of those dilapidated lighthouses crumbling on the coastline of Maine and stay up all night sending Morse code messages to the lonely and storm-tossed.

Of course, there's so much I never told you.

In February, I saw an old man on a park bench warming a frozen pigeon in his hands.

In September, I saw sparrows hovering over a churchyard, confused by the St. Francis scarecrow.

Robert Frost was afraid of the dark.

James Joyce was afraid of thunder.

While working the docks in New York City, Herman Melville daydreamed that one day he and Shakespeare would run into each other on the street and get drunk together on rum punch.

This was impossible, of course.

What is possible is that one day you and I will run into each other on the street and get drunk together on rum punch.

For now, all I can say is thank you.

Thank you for being my reader, my Third Man.

I think I'll leave you with this—a haiku to carry in the pocket of your winter coat along with your lighter and your lozenges.

In Japan, where New Year's Day was once considered to be everyone's birthday, the haiku masters were practically mandated to dash off a few lines to mark the occasion. At the turn of 1794, the poet Issa was far from home. He'd been wandering for years, sheltering in temples, braving every kind of weather in his tattered monk's robes. He was exactly halfway through his life, though of course he didn't know it. With a brush dipped in ink, he wrote in his bound journal:

New Year's Day—
what luck!
a clear blue sky

WORKS CITED

Ackroyd, Peter. *J.M.W. Turner: Ackroyd's Brief Lives*. New York: Knopf Doubleday Publishing Group, 2007.

Anastas, Benjamin. "The Foul Reign of Emerson's 'Self-Reliance.'" *New York Times*, December 2, 2011.

Audubon, John James. *The Birds of America, from Drawings Made in the United States and their Territories*. 7 vols. New York: J. J. Audubon; Philadelphia: J. B. Chevalier, 1840–1844. https://books.google.com/books?id=pnIDAAAAYAAJ&dq=The+Birds+of+America,+Volume+7++John+James+Audubon+1844.

———. *Journal of John James Audubon Made During His Trip to New Orleans in 1820–1821*. Edited by Howard Corning. Boston: Club of Odd Volumes, 1929. https://ia802606.us.archive.org/10/items/journalofjohnjam00audu/journalofjohnjam00audu.pdf.

Barrie, J. M. *Courage*. New York: Charles Scribner's Sons, 1922. http://www.gutenberg.org/files/10767/10767.txt.

Beckett, Samuel. *Stories and Texts for Nothing*. New York: Grove Press, 1967.

Bernstein, Jeremy. *Quantum Profiles*. Princeton: Princeton University Press, 1990.

Brassaï. *Conversations with Picasso*. Translated by Jane Marie Todd. Chicago: University of Chicago Press, 1999.

Byron, George Gordon Byron. *The Works of Lord Byron*. Edited by Ernest Hartley Coleridge. 6 vols. London: John Murray, 1898–1904. https://catalog.hathitrust.org/Record/100631646.

Chandler, Raymond. *Trouble Is My Business*. New York: Vintage, 1988.

Claffey, Jason. "More Wild Turkey Attacks in Brookline." *Patch*. November 25, 2014. http://patch.com/massachusetts/brookline/more-wild-turkey-attacks-brookline-0.

Clare, John. *John Clare's Autobiographical Writings*. Edited by Eric Robinson. Oxford: Oxford University Press, 1983.

Collins, Michael. *Carrying the Fire: An Astronaut's Journey*. New York: Farrar, Straus, and Giroux, 1974.

Crèvecœur, J. Hector St. John de. *Letters from an American Farmer and Other Essays*. Edited by Dennis D. Moore. Cambridge: Harvard University Press, 2013.

Delbanco, Andrew. "Melville Has Never Looked Better." *New York Times*, October 28, 2001.

Diamant, Kathi. *Kafka's Last Love: The Mystery of Dora Diamant*. New York: Basic Books, 2003.

Dickinson, Emily. *The Letters of Emily Dickinson*. Edited by Thomas H. Johnson and Theodora Van Wagenen Ward. 3 vols. Cambridge, MA: Harvard University Press, 1958.

——. *The Poems of Emily Dickinson*. Edited by Thomas H. Johnson. 3 vols. Cambridge, MA: Harvard University Press, 1955.

Doyle, Arthur Conan. *The New Annotated Sherlock Holmes*. 3 vols. Edited by Leslie S. Klinger. New York: W. W. Norton & Company, 2005.

Ellmann, Richard. *James Joyce*. New and Revised ed. Oxford: Oxford University Press, 1982.

Emerson, Ralph Waldo. *Emerson in His Journals*. Edited by Joel Porte. Cambridge, MA: Harvard University Press, 1984.

——. *Essays and Lectures*. Edited by Joel Porte. New York: Library of America, 1983.

Fitzgerald, F. Scott. *The Great Gatsby*. New York: Simon and Schuster, 2003.

Frost, Robert. *The Letters of Robert Frost to Louis Untermeyer*. Edited by Louis Untermeyer. New York: Holt, Rinehart, and Winston, 1963.

———. "Poetry and School." *The Atlantic Monthly*, June 1951.

Gauguin, Paul. *Paul Gauguin's Intimate Journals*. Translated by Van Wyck Brooks. Preface by Emil Gauguin. New York: Boni and Liveright, 1921. https://babel.hathitrust.org/cgi/pt?id=ucl. l0062371687.

Gehry, Frank. "A master architect asks, Now what?" Interview by Richard Saul Wurman. *TED2002*. https://www.ted.com/talks/frank_gehry_asks_then_what?.

Geiger, John. *The Third Man Factor: Surviving the Impossible*. New York: Weinstein Books, 2009.

Goldstein, Andrew. "Frank Gehry: I Don't Have a Leaking Problem, Okay?" *New York Magazine*. November 9, 2007. http://nymag.com/daily/intelligencer/2007/11/frank_gehry.html.

Grainger, Margaret, ed. *The Natural History Prose Writings of John Clare*. Oxford: Clarendon Press, 1983.

Haughton, Hugh, and Adam Phillips and Geoffrey Summerfield, eds. *John Clare in Context*. Cambridge, UK: Cambridge University Press, 1994.

Higginson, Thomas Wentworth. "Emily Dickinson's Letters." *The Atlantic Monthly,* October 1891.

Hoffmann, Yoel, ed. *Japanese Death Poems: Written by Zen Monks and Haiku Poets on the Verge of Dead*. Tokyo: Tuttle Publishing, 1986.

Howell, Elizabeth. "Apollo 11 Flight Log, July 21, 1969: Launching from the Moon." *Space.com*. July 21, 2014. http://www.space.com/26585-apollo-11-flight-log-july-21-1969.html.

Issa, Kobayashi. *Issa Zenshu*. Vol. 1. Edited by Shinano Kyōikukai. Nagano: Shinano Mainichi Shimbun-sha, 1976.

Keats, John. *John Keats: Selected Poems*. Edited by John Barnard. London: Penguin, 2007.

Lindbergh, Charles A. *The Spirit of St. Louis*. New York: Charles Scribner's Sons, 1953.

Melville, Herman. "Letter to Nathaniel Hawthorne, November [17?] 1851." *Melville.org*. http://www.melville.org/letter7.htm.

Meryman, Richard. "Andrew Wyeth: An Interview." *Life*, May 14, 1965.

Miller, Jason K. *Frank Gehry*. Edited by Susan Lauzau. New York: MetroBooks, 2002.

Mizener, Arthur. "Gatsby, 35 Years Later." *New York Times*, April 24, 1960.

Myerson, Joel. "Convers Francis and Emerson." *American Literature* 50:1 (March 1978): 17–36.

Nabokov, Vladimir. "The Vane Sisters." *The Hudson Review* 11.4 (Winter 1959).

——. *Vladimir Nabokov: Selected Letters 1940-1977*. Edited by Dmitri Nabokov and Matthew J. Bruccoli. New York: Houghton Mifflin Harcourt, 2012.

Nietzsche, Friedrich. *Basic Writings of Nietzsche*. Edited and translated by Walter Kaufmann. New York: Modern Library, 1968.

——. *Friedrich Nietzsches Briefe an Peter Gast*. Leipzig: Insel Verlag, 1908. https://babel.hathitrust.org/cgi/pt?id=hvd.hnnhjy.

Rimermay, Sara. "Putting a Smile on Sober Science." *New York Times*, May 13, 2004.

Salinger, J. D. *Nine Stories.* Boston: Little, Brown and Company, 1953.

Satie, Erik. "Mémoires d'un Amnésique: L'Intelligence et La Musicalité Chez Les Animaux," *La Revue Musicale S.I.M.* 10 (February 1, 1914): 69. http://bluemountain.princeton.edu/bluemtn/cgi-bin/bluemtn?a=d&d= bmtnabh19140201-01.2.26.

Shackleton, Ernest. *South: The Story of Shackleton's Last Expedition 1914-1917.* New York: The Macmillan Co., 1920. https://books.google.com/books?id=EICKclfgBPYC.

Shakespeare, William. *Romeo and Juliet.* Edited by J. A. Bryant, Jr. Signet Edition. New York: Penguin Group, 1998.

Shaw, Bernard. *Man and Superman.* Cambridge, MA: The University Press, 1903. http://www.bartleby.com/157.

Sisk, Bobby. "Complaints About Turkey Attacks On The Rise In Brookline." *Boston CBS.* November 21, 2012. http://boston.cbslocal.com/2012/11/21/turkey-complaints-on-the-rise-in-brookline/2012.

Tériade, E. "En causant avec Picasso." *L'Intransigéant,* June 15, 1932.

Thoreau, Henry David. *The Journal of Henry David Thoreau, 1837-1861.* Edited by Damion Searls. New York: New York Review of Books, 2011.

——. *The Portable Thoreau.* Edited by Jeffrey S. Cramer. New York: Penguin, 2012.

Twain, Mark. *Complete Works of Mark Twain.* East Sussex: Delphi Classics, 2013. Kindle edition.

Winthrop, John. *The Journal of John Winthrop, 1630 to 1649.* Edited by Richard S. Dunn, James Savage, and Laetitia Yeandle. Cambridge, MA: Harvard University Press, 1996.

Woolf, Virginia. *The Diary of Virginia Woolf.* 5 vols. Edited by Anne Olivier Bell, assisted by Andrew McNeillie. London: Hogarth Press, 1979-1985.

——. "On Being Ill." *The Criterion*, January, 1926.

——. *The Virginia Woolf Reader.* Edited by Mitchell A. Leaska. New York: Harcourt, 1984.

——. *A Writer's Diary.* Edited by Leonard Woolf. New York: Houghton Mifflin Harcourt, 2003.

Wordsworth, William. *The Complete Poetical Works.* London: Macmillan and Co., 1888. http://www.bartleby.com/145.

Wyndham, Joan. *Love is Blue: A Wartime Diary.* London: Heinemann, 1986.

ACKNOWLEDGMENTS

Many essays in this collection appeared on *The Drunken Odyssey*, a website and podcast dedicated to the writing life. Grateful thanks to the editor, John King.

Thanks as well to Jodi Burrel, Chris Dowd, and Jim Dowd, and to the Etruscan team: Phil Brady, Bill Schneider, and the tireless Pamela Turchin.

I am especially grateful to Suzanne Matson, my teacher and friend, and to my mother, Karen Dowd, my sounding board and spare eyes.

PUBLISHER ACKNOWLEDGMENTS

Brassaï, *Conversations with Picasso*. Translated by Jane Marie Todd. Copyright © 1999 The University of Chicago. Originally published as *Conversations avec Picasso* text and photographs © Gilberte Brassai and Editions Gallimard, 1964, 1997. Reprinted by permission of The University of Chicago Press.

Excerpt from *Emily Dickinson: Selected Letters*, edited by Thomas H. Johnson, Cambridge, Mass.: The Belknap Press of Harvard University Press, Copyright © 1958, 1971, 1986 by the President and Fellows of Harvard College. Copyright © 1914, 1924, 1932 by Martha Dickinson Bianchi.

Excerpt from *The Poems of Emily Dickinson: Reading Edition*, edited by Ralph W. Franklin, Cambridge, Mass.: The Belknap Press of Harvard University Press, Copyright © 1998, 1999 by the President and Fellows of Harvard College. Copyright © 1951, 1955 by the President and Fellows of Harvard College. Copyright © renewed 1979, 1983 by the President and Fellows of Harvard College. Copyright © 1914, 1918, 1919, 1924, 1929, 1930, 1932, 1935, 1937, 1942 by Martha Dickinson Bianchi. Copyright © 1952, 1957, 1958, 1963, 1965 by Mary L. Hampson.

ABOUT THE AUTHOR

WILL DOWD WAS born in Braintree, Massachusetts. He earned a BA from Boston College, as a Presidential Scholar; an MS from MIT, as a John Lyons Fellow; and an MFA in Creative Writing from New York University, as a Jacob K. Javits Fellow. His writing and art have appeared in numerous magazines. He lives in the Boston area.

Books from Etruscan Press

Etruscan Press is Proud of Support Received from

Wilkes University

Youngstown State University

The Ohio Arts Council

The Stephen & Jeryl Oristaglio Foundation

The Nathalie & James Andrews Foundation

The National Endowment for the Arts

The Ruth H. Beecher Foundation

The Bates-Manzano Fund

The New Mexico Community Foundation

Drs. Barbara Brothers & Gratia Murphy Fund

The Rayen Foundation

The Pella Corporation

The Raymond John Wean Foundation

Founded in 2001 with a generous grant from the Oristaglio Foundation, Etruscan Press is a nonprofit cooperative of poets and writers working to produce and promote books that nurture the dialogue among genres, achieve a distinctive voice, and reshape the literary and cultural histories of which we are a part.

etruscan press

www.etruscanpress.org

Etruscan Press books may be ordered from

Consortium Book Sales and Distribution

800.283.3572

www.cbsd.com

Etruscan Press is a 501(c)(3) nonprofit organization.
Contributions to Etruscan Press are tax deductible
as allowed under applicable law.
For more information, a prospectus,
or to order one of our titles,
contact us at books@etruscanpress.org.